Redoing Gender

"In this, one of the first studies of people who identify as nonbinary, Helana Darwin masterfully balances the voices of her participants with an astute sociological analysis. Not only does this book provide important insight into how people who identify as nonbinary understand their identities and navigate social relationships, it also has much to say about doing, undoing, and redoing gender for everyone regardless of gender identity. This book is an important contribution to our sociological understanding of gender."

—Mimi Schippers, Professor and Chair, *Department of Sociology, Gender & Sexuality Studies Program, Tulane University, USA*

"At a time when we are simultaneously experiencing increasing visibility of nonbinary genders and legal and physical violence against gender non-conforming people, *Redoing Gender* provides a timely exploration of changing conceptions of gender beyond the cis/trans binary. Darwin asks key questions, like how nonbinary people achieve their gender in a society that denies and erases their existence through accountability structures. In doing this, she reengages the foundational *doing gender theory* in an accessible manner, allowing us to reimagine the possibilities of gender in the first place. This text is an invaluable resource to scholars, policy makers, activists, and the public alike."

—Megan Nanney, *East Carolina University, USA, and Chair of Sociologists for Trans Justice*

"*Redoing Gender* boldly shines a spotlight on nonbinary experiences in what is a significant contribution to trans studies. Darwin's *Redoing Gender* is a necessary addition to the literature on gender and sex in the current era. Our interactions and institutions must shift in order to make room for nonbinary bodies, identities, and experiences. Darwin carves out a space for *doing gender theory* to grow in ways that expect rather than accommodate gender diversity. Darwin has proven herself to be an astute contender in the theoretical arena. This book offers us a new paradigm for understanding gender, and our relationship to and experience of it, while lifting up the experiences of nonbinary people who perhaps have the most at stake in this gender revolution. Academics, cisgender and binary trans allies, and those working with trans and nonbinary populations are sure to benefit from engaging with this text."

—Austin Johnson, Assistant Professor of Sociology, *Kenyon College, USA*

D1489783

Helana Darwin

Redoing Gender

How Nonbinary Gender Contributes Toward Social Change

Helana Darwin
New York, NY, USA

ISBN 978-3-030-83616-0   ISBN 978-3-030-83617-7   (eBook)
https://doi.org/10.1007/978-3-030-83617-7

Cover design by eStudioCalamar

This Palgrave Macmillan imprint is published by the registered company Springer Nature Switzerland AG
The registered company address is: Gewerbestrasse 11, 6330 Cham, Switzerland

This book is dedicated to gender nonbinary people everywhere

Acknowledgments

This book has been quite the journey, beginning in 2013 with a class assignment and culminating in 2021 with my first book. As I wrote my dissertation and then revised it into this book form, I also published three academic journal articles from the same data. Thus, I owe a massive debt of gratitude to the various editors and anonymous peer reviewers who provided me with feedback on my article manuscripts along the way. Their thought-provoking nudges helped me hone the main arguments that I present in this book. I must also thank all the faculty members who took the time to read and edit this book when it was in dissertation form, specifically Kadji Amin, Katy Fallon, Catherine Marrone, Mimi Schippers, and Tiffany Joseph. And thank you to Stony Brook University for the Turner Dissertation Award, which partially funded this project.

I couldn't have completed this research without the participation of my interviewees or the help of my research assistants. Thank you to everyone who answered my call for respondents. I did not have any money to offer you in compensation for your time, but you participated anyway and amazed me with your generosity. I hope you feel like your time and emotional investment was worthwhile and I hope you benefit in some way from this project. Even though my institution refused my request to use people's real names who wanted credit for their stories, I give my full support to those who decide to claim credit for their contributions after this book's publication. You deserve the option of including it on your resumes, as co-creators of the collective knowledge that I present in these pages. Thank you also to an amazing team of undergraduate students who helped me transcribe audio files, edit transcripts, and meet to discuss emergent themes. This team includes: Talissa Tejada, Jessica Shvarts, Shauna Scholl, Moyse Romane, Shivanshu Prasad, Fayik Nouri, Savannah Moran, Kimberly Moonsammy, Rebecca Molino, Christine Ferrer, Allilsa Fernandez, Sandra Cuccia, Angelina Lange, and Emilio Castillo.

Thank you to my spiritual home LabShul and its founder and Rabbi Amichai Lau-Lavie for running a Jewish community that is actively centered on social justice issues and LGBTQIA+ inclusivity. I have had so many wonderful conversations with congregants about the gender binary system while writing this book. Thank you also to the various establishments in my neighborhood that provided outlets outside of my home where I could do work before the pandemic. This includes Darling Coffee, Buunni Coffee, Inwood Local, and Buddha Beer Bar.

I have benefitted enormously from several writing workshop groups while revising my articles and book manuscript. Thank you to Penny Harvey and TehQuinn Forbes for feedback on my articles. Thank you to Landon Schnabel, Elizabeth Mount, and Ilana Horowitz for the in-depth and invaluable feedback on my book proposal and each chapter of this book. Having the support of community during this strange transitional time between graduating from my doctoral program and beginning my career has been amazing. You all have been such a source of comfort and stability in my life. And you are all incredibly brilliant. Thank you so much.

I am also grateful to the anonymous peer reviewers at Palgrave-Macmillan and my editor, Nina Guttapalle. Thank you for giving me a chance as a first-time author. Of all the book editors I met throughout this contract-shopping process, Nina has been the most supportive and encouraging of the book that I wanted to create. It is a tricky book to market, since it is academic in one sense and very straightforward in another. Much like nonbinary gender itself, my book does not fit into the arbitrarily binary book marketing system. I could have forced this book to be something it wasn't, in order to make it fit more easily into the academic book genre, but it wouldn't have felt right. Nonbinary gender is confusing enough to cisgender people—I wanted this book to demystify it, which would have been difficult if I was obligated to use dense theoretical jargon and overly engage with scholarly discussions. Thank you, Nina, for gambling on our success in marketing this unique book and for recognizing the value of its subject matter.

On a personal note, I owe a massive debt of gratitude to my amazing husband and co-parent Matthew Zimmer. I would not have made it to the finish line without the various forms of support that he has provided. I want to specify these forms of labor to clarify how much teamwork is required for a parent to publish a dissertation-turned-book. Matt has helped tirelessly with childcare and domestic demands that have arisen throughout the course of this project. He stayed home alone with the children for days on end while I flew away to conferences. He altered his work schedule when necessary to pick up or drop off children when I needed to attend classes or events. He learned how to cook by necessity during the many nights when he played "single dad." When our child began to struggle because he missed his mommy on the many nights when I had to sleep on an air mattress in my office, Matt held him for hours to soothe him to sleep. I also relied on Matt throughout the years as the last reader before I submitted articles for publication. He helped me edit for clarity of content and fixed minute grammatical and spelling errors that escaped my attention. His feedback has been instrumental to my manuscripts' polish. In so many ways, he has been in my corner, on Team Helana, through thick and thin. I love you, Matt. Thank you for helping me have it all.

Finally, I must express my gratitude to my children, Micah and Milo, for the sacrifices they made while I conducted this research and wrote this book. I sure hope you won't remember how busy and stressed out your mama was during your young years of life, but I know that this project compromised my ability to be as present and attentive as I wished to be. I hope you forgive me for getting the work-life balance wrong at times. Raising you two has been such an adventure and given me so much valuable insight into the gender binary system. I will always advocate for your freedom of self-expression. Be you, play with gender, discard gender, whatever. I will support you and love you throughout your gender journeys. I just want you to feel at home in your own skin.

What Are Your Pronouns?

You can easily find my own in my email signature or the bio sections of my social media profiles. You might find them literally attached to my body in the form of a lapel pin, button, or name-tag if you catch me in the right setting. And, since March of 2020, you can find them in my handle for Zoom or any other web-based video conferencing software that I use for most face-to-face interactions. I teach Sociology at a private institution in the Midwest region of the United States and it is common practice at our small liberal arts college for faculty, staff, and students to declare their pronouns at the start of each semester and to include them in email signatures. Pronoun rounds have become compulsory practice in my circles and I would guess that I am not the first stranger to ask you to disclose your own.

The understanding of gender identity as a potentially shifting experience has quickly moved into mainstream discourse and the social institutions through which it circulates. The most obvious sign of this cultural shift is our public awareness and discussion of *pronouns*. Pronoun queries, along-side other public displays of allyship, in everything from college classroom roll calls to hospital intake forms, suggest that individuals and institutions are welcoming this gender revolution. This suggestion, as *Redoing Gender* demonstrates, is misleading.

In order to ensure that the revolution leaves no gender behind, it is vital that we look beyond public displays of inclusivity to closely examine the ways that institutions expect, accommodate, and adapt to gender diversity or fail to do so in their everyday practices. Through its attention to the lived experiences and material conditions of those on the outside of the gender binary, *Redoing Gender* reminds us that a shift in the content of gender categories, and the subsequent widening of the net cast for the bodies and experiences that may be contained within, do not necessarily equate to or result in a shift in the form of a hegemonic binary gender system. In disrupting the gender binary, it is more difficult for nonbinary people to assimilate into both cisnormative and transnormative institutions and interactions. Rather, interactions and institutions must shift their orientation to gender as a binary system and make way for a diversity of identities, bodies, and experiences.

Darwin has proven herself to be an astute contender in the theoretical arena, carving out space for trans/gender theory to grow in ways that include both those shifting within and those breaking from binary gender categories. *Redoing Gender*, in what is a necessary contribution to *doing gender theory*, goes beyond the inclusion of gender diversity to the radical reorientation of gender theory in order to focus on and build from nonbinary gender experience. In building a theory of gender from outside of the binary, we are offered a better view of its structure, its modes of empowerment, and its means of constraint for all genders. A nonbinary approach to gender theory offers a new perspective, and a critical standpoint, for understanding and perhaps redoing gender and our relationship to and experience of it. More than that, it lifts up the experiences of nonbinary people, who perhaps have the most at stake in the contemporary gender revolution.

Austin H. Johnson
Kenyon College, Gambier, USA

Contents

Abbreviations

AFAB	Assigned Female a Birth
AMAB	Assigned Male at Birth
DFAB	Designated Female at Birth
DMAB	Designated Male at Birth
GNC	Gender Non-Conforming
GQ	Genderqueer
HRT	Hormone Replacement Therapy
NB	Nonbinary
T	Testosterone

Introduction

"Hey! Hey Lady! Is it a boy or a girl? It's a boy, right?" I was used to this type of question from strangers by this point in my pregnancy. Typically, people did not shout this at me from across a room, however, and I was turned off by this man's aggression. I began my cumbersome climb up the stairs, staring resolutely at my phone, pretending I didn't hear him. All the while, he shouted "Hey Lady!" Finally, he gave up and announced confidently and loudly to no one in particular "It's a boy."

Why did this strange man feel so entitled to know the gender of my unborn baby? And did he really want to know its gender or its genitals? Clearly for him, these two things were one and the same, but they are actually quite different. Though I knew from ultrasounds that my baby had a penis, I also knew that this anatomical part did not determine their gender. My baby might identify as a boy/man some day in the future, but they could also identify as a woman or reject these rigid gender categories altogether and eventually "come out" as nonbinary. Asking me whether my unborn baby was a boy or a girl was a nonstarter for me; the only answer I could possibly give in good faith to end the conversation quickly would be "I don't know." Or if I felt daring, "I won't know until they're old enough to tell me."

The timing has been strange—writing this book while pregnant and then while toting around a gender-ambiguous newborn. My commitment to challenging society's investment in the gender binary comes to the fore many more times a day than it would otherwise. After all, I am (more or less) a feminine cisgender woman. In my daily life, very little triggers any sense of

H. Darwin, *Redoing Gender*,
https://doi.org/10.1007/978-3-030-83617-7_1

gender dysphoria for me. I am extremely privileged compared to the people I interviewed for this book. And my awareness of that privilege, compounded by my familiarity with the pain that the current system produces for those who identify as neither men nor women, turns these seemingly harmless interactions with the public into fraught moments for me.

"Why can't you just be polite and answer the stranger? He's obviously just trying to be nice," my former advisor once asked when I relayed the afore-mentioned anecdote. A million possible responses raced through my head. First, this man was not being "nice" by holding me forcefully accountable to the gender binary system and aggressively demanding to know the gender or the genital status of the small human inside of me. This stranger might have been enacting an interactive script that is considered "polite" in our cisnor-mative society, but it wasn't polite by my estimation, nor is it considered polite by my nonbinary interviewees. Manners are inherently political, reflec-tive of the values of the most powerful people in a society. Where to start, while explaining why I cannot in good conscience go along with this "polite" script....

Positionality

I was initially forced to confront my investment in binary gender ideology when a trans woman asked to join the weekly women's spirituality circle that I held at my Liberal Arts college. After conferring with the other members, we agreed that it was a nonissue and she became an integral part of our commu-nity. Nevertheless, I continued to create these binary gender-segregated rituals. In fact, my unquestioning—and inherently political—commitment to holding these circles continued until the summer after I graduated from college, when I worked as seasonal staff at a Jewish retreat center. I assumed that my coworkers would be enthusiastic about a monthly women's new moon circle, since such gatherings are built into Jewish tradition (known as Rosh Chodesh rituals), and I was absolutely dismayed by their luke-warm response. Embarrassingly, I remember shedding actual cis tears about people's lack of engagement with this endeavor. Finally, a few of the seasonal farming interns confronted me about the exclusionary impact of my efforts, explaining that many of them identified as nonbinary—that is, they did not identify as men *or* women, trans men *or* trans women, but as another gender configuration entirely, sometimes called genderqueer or genderfluid. At the time of this intervention I reacted defensively, arguing for women's space on a biological and essentialist basis, citing our presumably universal experiences of menstruation, socialization, and sexuality. I even managed to feel victimized by this confrontation and continued to feel defensive about it years later when I took my first courses in Transgender Studies at the remarkably queer Union Theological Seminary. However, despite my initial resistance, this information percolated within my brain over the years. Eventually I became more sensitive to the pain that cis women like myself had inflicted upon transgender and nonbinary communities. Thereafter, I began to feel uneasy about my complicity with the binary gender ideology that undergirds women's spirituality culture and stopped hosting gender-segregated rituals.

These realizations (among others) motivated me to leave religious studies for sociology. Yet as I became increasingly familiar with the sociology of gender, I was struck by the literature's unyielding focus on power differentials between cis women and cis men, as though other genders do not exist. I was particularly troubled by our overreliance on these binary frameworks within presumably universally applicable analytical models such as Candace West and Don Zimmerman's (1987) massively influential "doing gender" model. How do people "do gender" beyond the binary, if they are neither men nor women, I wondered.

This guiding interest propelled me to embark upon this research project. Problematically, there was precious little sociological literature on nonbinary gender when I began this journey in 2013. To my understanding, my preliminary virtual ethnography "Doing Gender Beyond the Binary" (2017) and stef shuster's "Punctuating Accountability" (2017) were the first two sociological articles to explicitly analyze nonbinary gender through qualitative research methods.[1] Since then, a diverse and rich body of literature has emerged within sociology, psychology, and gender studies that focuses on nonbinary particularities. For example, while analyzing narratives of transgender authenticity, Garrison (2018) found that nonbinary transgender interviewees worried that they were somehow "not trans enough" to claim the transgender label.[2] Sumerau and Mathers (2019) further observed that their nonbinary transgender survey respondents reported resistance from cisgender people as well as the LGBTQIA+ community when they laid claim to the transgender label.[3] The authors conceptualize this finding as evidence of how people engage in a gatekeeping practice that shuster (2019) calls "othering the other."[4] Elsewhere, sociologists have debated whether nonbinary gender should even be analyzed as an identity, as opposed to a gender construction that is shaped by the binary gender structure.[5] This nonbinary gender studies corpus continues to grow exponentially, as more literature is available to draw upon.

I have done my best to stay up to date on this literature. However, since this book project took shape before this surge in interest, very little of it informed my approach, guiding interests, or analytical insights. It would be a bit disingenuous to retroactively insert references to it now that the book is complete. I developed my analysis mainly from my interviewees' own words, which I block quote with wild abandon, much to some peer reviewers' chagrin.

But that's okay. I am not writing this book as an offering to the oftentimes all-too-insular academy. I am writing it because I know how to speak to fellow cisgender people in a way that will hopefully help them get past the type of resistance to nonbinary gender that I also used to feel. My primary hope is that the rich descriptions I include of nonbinary people's lives and experiences will elicit compassion from those who feel protective of the gender binary, like I did in the past; people who resist the singular "they" pronoun on grammatical grounds or who worry that the shift toward phrases like "people who menstruate" will somehow detract from the fight for women's rights. Of course, readers will approach this book with a range of preexisting opinions, attitudes, and ideologies. However, I also assume that readers would only bother to access this book if they wanted to understand the alleged "gender revolution" that the media extols.

All that being said, this book is not only for cisgender readers. I imagine that transgender, nonbinary, and gender non-conforming readers will also benefit from the opportunity to compare and contrast their gender experiences with those of the people featured in this book. Nonbinary and transgender people who are further along in their gender journeys may not learn much from this book, but many others who are newer to the process of questioning their gender will undoubtedly find value within the rich descriptions of everyday life that I go out of my way to feature in the following pages.

I do not claim to know more about the experiences in this book than the gender-diverse people who live it every day. What I can do is offer a sociological analysis of the interactional processes that nonbinary people perform on a daily basis to achieve social recognition. These processes are of the utmost significance to sociology, insofar as they nudge our resistant society toward an expanded understanding of gender that acknowledges gender diversity. These microscale psychological and interactional processes illuminate the mechanisms that drive social change, and ultimately "redo" gender as cisgender people knew it.

Terminology

Before going any further, I'd like to take a moment to provide definitions and explanations that will help you enter the world of nonbinary people. I include footnotes that provide additional information and resources about gender/labeling politics for readers who would like to know more.

Transgender—People who move away from the gender that was assigned to them at birth are generally categorized as "transgender." Most typically, the word "transgender" is associated with trans men and trans women, who transitioned from woman to man or from man to woman. A broader understanding of "transgender" includes all gender-variant people.[6] I explore the complexity of transgender-labeling later.

Cisgender—Until relatively recently, transgender people were marked as "other" through the trans prefix while everyone else got to remain unmarked as just people. This lopsided labeling dynamic eventually gave way to the increasingly common practice of specifying non-transgender people as "cisgender." The cis prefix was chosen as a corollary to the trans prefix, because they are both Latin and have opposite meanings. "Trans" means to cross, while "cis" means to remain in place. Thus, men and women who were assigned those genders at birth are "cis men" and "cis women."[7]

Nonbinary— Nonbinary people are those with genders that are too complicated to place in the "man" or "woman" category. Some experience their gender as both, some as neither, some as fluid and changing. Sometimes nonbinary people identify as transgender, but not always, as we will examine in more depth later.[8]

Genderqueer—Just as some identify as sexually queer, others identify as genderqueer. This label is oftentimes used interchangeably with nonbinary, though some maintain that there are important differences, which we will also get to later. In my 2014 call for interviewees, I used both of these terms (nonbinary and genderqueer) since at that time survey data[9] indicated that they were the most popular gender labels besides "man," "woman," "trans man," and "trans woman."

AFAB—Assigned Female at Birth (or sometimes DFAB—"Designated Female at Birth") is a way to specify the binary sex/gender category that was officially applied to a nonbinary individual when they were born—without implying that the gender assignment was valid or applicable today. I refer to these designations ONLY when a stark pattern emerges in my interviewees' experiences based on the sex/gender (these two are often conflated in the social imagination) that was assigned to them at birth. These birth assignments tend to dictate people's early experiences of socialization and gender conditioning,[10] as well as their early efforts to make sense of their sexuality.

AMAB—Assigned Male at Birth (sometimes called DMAB). See Above.

HRT—Hormone Replacement Therapy (HRT) is a popular medical procedure among nonbinary people. AMAB people can take testosterone blockers and estrogen supplements to feel and look less masculine and AFAB people can take testosterone to feel and look less feminine. Not all nonbinary people feel a need or desire to pursue HRT. It can be difficult for nonbinary people to acquire these treatments due to medical and psychological diagnostic criteria that assumes that anyone who is not cis is a trans man or a trans woman.[11] We will explore this institutionalization of the gender binary in more depth later.

Misgendering—Misgendering is the interaction wherein someone projects the wrong gender onto someone else. Being called a woman or a man when you are not a woman or a man—and perhaps have worked very hard to distance yourself from those gender categories—can be very upsetting.[12] "Upsetting" is actually too understated of a word choice here, since constant misgendering contributes toward suicidal ideation among some of my interviewees, as this book will discuss. Misgendering is an extremely pervasive experience for nonbinary people within the binary gender system, in part due to our binary-gendered linguistic structure. Sometimes instead of "misgendering," I will use the more sociological phrase "misrecognition,"[13] which more accurately places culpability upon the person who is making the erroneous gender attribution.

Pronouns—Just like man and woman are not in fact the only gender categories, he/him/his and she/her/hers are not the only pronoun clusters that people use to refer to themselves. Some people feel uncomfortable using these pronouns (usually due to their gender identity) and must become more inventive. The most commonly used alternative pronoun is the singular "they," as in "they left their umbrella in the shop." This usage of "they," to refer to someone with an unknown gender, has a long-standing history within the English language.[14] Thus, it is the obvious choice for many nonbinary people who don't want to use the binary-gendered alternatives. This is not to say that ALL nonbinary people use they/them/their as their pronouns. Some people identify as nonbinary while feeling apathetic toward pronouns, or actively choose to use one of the binary options. The reasoning for this varies and we will revisit this later. For now, just know that I use the pronouns as specified by people who I interviewed and most use they/them/their.

Methods

Again, when I began this research in 2014 there was virtually no social scientific research on nonbinary gender.[15] Gender studies research occasionally mentioned nonbinary gender, but almost always offhandedly as a subset of transgender. Thankfully, a few large-scale surveys on transgender people had recently been published that permitted nonbinary/genderqueer people to announce themselves through write-in options for gender labels.[16] These reports indicated that nonbinary people have a different experience in society than trans men and trans women, but could not offer explanations for these differences. Furthermore, the data within these studies only reflected the experiences of transgender people who answered the call for respondents—some of whom happened to identify as nonbinary or genderqueer in addition to transgender. This sampling strategy excluded by design any nonbinary or genderqueer people who did not consider themselves transgender. My desire to learn more about nonbinary people's experiences in society required original research.

I wanted to interview nonbinary people about their experiences in a binary gendered society, but I didn't know for sure what questions to ask. I could barely even perform a traditional literature review due to the dearth of directly relevant extant research. Meanwhile, in virtual chatrooms across the Internet, nonbinary people were meeting on a regular basis to discuss their experiences of daily life. Therefore, I logically decided to start my project in one such public site, lurking and observing the main themes that emerged in the community members' discussions. Perhaps unsurprisingly, virtual spaces have become important resources for those who study geographically disparate or hard to reach populations, including—but not limited to—Lesbian/Gay/Bisexual/Transgender/Queer groups.[17] Scholars have noted that such online communities provide a "safe space," or a Goffmanian "backstage space,"[18] where marginalized individuals can acquire support from one another and develop their sense of collective identity.[19]

In order to respect users' privacy, I selected a forum that encourages anonymity: Reddit. While reading through discussion threads, it became quickly apparent that there is no one way to be, look, or "do" nonbinary gender.[20] This gender category is simply too diverse to satisfy social scientists' compulsive desire to produce orderly typifications. In this sense, it forces us to rethink gender (and gender theory) altogether. Sure, some nonbinary people identify as transgender, but some do not; some think of gender as an identity and some do not; some believe there are rigid definitions and rules for group membership and some do not. Within the discussion threads, I surmised that there is an intragroup tension around whether one must "look" nonbinary in order to prove that one is authentically nonbinary, as well as controversies over what even constitutes the "nonbinary look." I also witnessed warmth, compassion, and support for fellow nonbinary people who turn to the site for advice on how to contend with obstacles such as "coming out," workplace discrimination, gaining access to medical care, and expressing themselves to others. People turned to the group to share the highs in life, such as victories over discrimination, as well as the lows such as suicidal ideation.

This study helped me create a list of questions that I would later ask nonbinary people to expound upon within interviews. My questions aimed to trace the contours of the gender binary system, by exploring the obstacles that nonbinary people encounter in their identity formulation, bodies, relationships, and interactions with institutions. The full "interview script" reads as follows.

Interview Script

VERBAL ASSENT
Hello! Thank you for taking the time to Skype with me today. Have you had a chance to read the consent form and do you have any questions? Is it okay with you if I take an audio recording of our interview, so I can transcribe it afterward?

PRONOUNS
To start, will you please tell me what gender label you use and what pronouns I should use when addressing you?
Why is this the pronoun you use? What about "she" or "woman" doesn't feel right to you? What about "he" or "man" doesn't feel right to you?
Have you used other pronouns in the past? Have you considered any other pronouns? How did you learn about these other pronouns?
Do other people call you by these pronouns? If so, who? How do people react when you ask them to call you by these pronouns? Does anyone refuse to use them? Is there anyone you have not informed of your wishes? Who? Why haven't you asked them to?
Can you please tell me about your experience with surveys and documentation that make you select man or woman? How does it feel to have to choose one? Have you ever had a service or good denied to you unless you selected one? Have you taken surveys that included additional options?

IDENTITY

When did you first begin to question your gender identity? What was happening in your life at that time? How did you experiment with this new identity and learn more about it?

When did you first come out to people, if you have yet? Who did you come out to first? How did they react? Are there spheres where you are more comfortable being out than others?

Why aren't you out to the people who still do not know? What do you think would happen if you came out to them?

Are you a member of any queer groups or do you attend queer events? Do you participate in queer discussions or groups on the Internet? If so which ones? What do you get out of this engagement? Do you feel included in the LGBTQIA+ scene? Is there any way it could be more inclusive to genderqueer individuals?

Have you ever experienced any physical threats for being genderqueer? Unwanted sexual attention?

WORK

What do you do for a living? Are you out about being genderqueer? How do people respond?

What jobs have you held since coming out as genderqueer?

Have you ever experienced discrimination of any sort for being genderqueer?

DRESS

I'm curious as to how you express your identity through clothing. Please walk me through any wardrobe shifts you've made.

How do you shop for clothes?

How do you like to dress on formal occasions? At work? On the beach?

How do people react to you in these clothes?

Has anyone ever told you to dress differently? Bosses, partners, parents, etc. Gendered dress codes at school, work, etc.

Why? Did you do it? Why or why not?

SEXUALITY

How would you describe your sexual orientation? Has it changed over the years? Did you come out to people about your sexuality?

I'm curious about how the process of coming out as your sexual identity compares or contrasts with coming out as genderqueer. Will you please explain it to me?

How has coming out as genderqueer affected your dating life, if at all?

BODY

Have you made any changes to your body since coming out to yourself about being genderqueer? Through binding, packing, hair cutting, shaving/not shaving, hormones, surgeries, makeup, bra-stuffing, etc.? Would you ever consider transitioning?

Why have you made these changes? Do people react to you differently now? If so, how?

Do you experience any issues with public restrooms or sex-segregated changing rooms?

Have you ever been involved in team sports?

RELIGION

Are you a part of any religion? If so, can you tell me a little about how people in your religious community have reacted to your gender expression?

What do you do with liturgical pronouns? How do you feel about G-d language? Are there any binary rituals or activities that require you to pick the male or female option? Which do you choose and why?

MISC:

How do children react to you? Do they assume you are one gender or the other? Have you ever tried to explain your gender identity to them? How did that go?

How has your race/ethnicity affected your experiences as a genderqueer person?

Have you traveled much? Was it easier or harder to be genderqueer in one place compared to another? If so, how?

Do you have any disabilities or neuro-divergences that I should know about? (if it hasn't already been specified) How old are you?

Do you have any siblings? If yes, are you out to them? How did they react?

How would you identify your socioeconomic class?

Is there anything else you would like to share with me about your experience or your identity?

Follow-Up Interviews

Four years after conducting these interviews, I invited people to answer my questions again. I decided to do this when one of my interviewees told me that their gender identity, thoughts, and experiences had changed so much over that four-year time span that their answers would likely be quite different. I decided this would be an interesting way to check in on their gender journeys, and any changes in society, with regards to how easy or difficult it is to be nonbinary. Since the four-year gap between interviews happened to correspond almost exactly with the Trump administration, I added one new section:

POLITICS
How have you been since Trump was elected?
Have you experienced any increased hostility or discrimination?
Are there any policies you're concerned about?

I didn't want the original interview responses to influence people's responses the second time around, so I decided not to send them their original interview transcript beforehand. However, I did send it to them afterward, along with my encouragement to reply with any thoughts they had on how their gender identity/experience has changed or stayed the same.

Interview Sample

Before I could ask any interview questions, I had to find people to interview. This proved to be remarkably difficult, as with any hard to reach population.[21] At first I relied upon word-of-mouth advertising among nonbinary people whom I knew. Once people began to reach out to me, I asked them to share my call for respondents within their social media networks as well as within their friend groups. Through this "snowball sampling" method I eventually collected interviews from forty-seven people.[22] However, it took a year and a half for me to collect these interviews and I struggled to recruit many people of color, despite my best efforts. This limitation is unfortunate, and likely inextricable from my positionality as a white researcher, my reliance upon snowball sampling (due to a lack of resources), and my inability to compensate interviewees for their time. Tellingly, I received several emails throughout the course of this project inquiring into payment; when I replied that there was none, I never heard back from these people. My study is also limited by my reliance on the Internet for advertising and communicating with interviewees. This might have skewed my sample toward a young middle-class demographic that has access to the Internet and uses it for social interaction. I fervently hope that future researchers are able to recruit samples that are more diverse. Such samples would undoubtedly illuminate additional themes and psychological and social processes beyond what I cover in this book.

I also did not receive as many follow-up interview volunteers as I anticipated. In the end, I collected responses from 22 people, which amounted to approximately half of my original sample. It is difficult to say why I only heard back from half of them. The timing worked out such that these conversations coincided with the beginning of coronavirus lockdown efforts, between March and April of 2020. Some people warned me that they were already burned out on video conferencing, although others seemed quite eager for the human connection. I also know that some never received my emails because of their deactivated email addresses. It's further possible that some people no longer identified as nonbinary and thus didn't feel comfortable participating in the study anymore. I'll never know for certain why I only heard back from half and whether this half replied for any specific reason. I couldn't detect any such common denominator when I analyzed the text from our interviews.

Despite these limitations, this study also has considerable strengths. By combining data from my virtual ethnography with my in-depth interviews, I have been able to assess the social issues with which nonbinary people contend on a broad scale and subsequently highlight the lived experiences of these social issues in rich detail. My sample is geographically disparate due to my utilization of Skype in the interview stage, resulting in my ability to compare interpersonal and institutional discrimination within different regions and even offer some tentative observations about differences between countries. However, the vast majority of my interviewees are from the United States and I only offer observations about differences at the national level when it pertains to healthcare systems.

This book includes people with all gender expressions and pronouns. They are from all over the United States and a few are even from other countries, including Iceland, Denmark, Russia, Canada, Bangladesh, France, Germany, Norway, and Argentina. Interviewees from within the United States were distributed across the country's regions. Their ages range from 19 to 61 with an average age of 26. The majority have a college-level education and are white—which is not necessarily representative of the broader nonbinary population, though we would need better large-scale data to know this for certain. Two-thirds were assigned female at birth, one-third male at birth, and one person is intersex. Some have disabilities, such as chronic pain, fibromyalgia, hearing loss, and polycystic ovarian syndrome. Many have mental health conditions such as depression, anxiety, and post-traumatic stress syndrome. Several are neuro-divergent with diagnoses such as autism and bipolar disorder. They hail from varied religious backgrounds including Judaism, Islam, and (majority) Christianity. Some have changed their bodies to reflect their gender, but not all; some identify as transgender, but not all. The one thing they all have in common is a sense of group membership in the gender category "nonbinary" or "genderqueer."

Analysis

I used a grounded theory approach while analyzing these transcripts. I read each transcript at least four times throughout my manual coding and analytical processes. I read each one the first time to check for transcription errors and a second time for thematic content. I then conducted line by line open-coding to determine the variety of topics and themes that emerged within each interview.[23] I checked these results against the analytical memos that my research assistants recorded and we discussed the main themes during bimonthly meetings. Finally, I performed a round of closed coding, which condensed open codes into broader thematic and processual categories.[24] Once I completed this process, I looked for any noteworthy differences between respondents based on relevant demographic information (such as nationality, gender assigned at birth, race, or sexuality). I noted particularly strong differences between people's experiences based on the sex/gender assigned to them at birth and their regionality/nationality. Fewer differences emerged along racial lines, although this is likely a reflection of my whiteness as a researcher as it impacted my sampling and my respondents' willingness to discuss race.

Notes

1. Darwin (2017) and shuster (2017).
2. Garrison.
3. Sumerau and Mathers (2019).
4. Shuster (2019).
5. Risman (2019) and Barbee and Schrock (2019).
6. For more on transgender labeling politics, see Darwin's (2020) "Challenging the Cisgender/Transgender Binary: Nonbinary People and the Transgender Label"; Catalano (2015) "'Trans Enough?' The Pressures Trans Men Negotiate in Higher Education"; Davidson (2007) "Seeking Refuge Under the Umbrella: Inclusion, Exclusion, and Organizing Within the Category Transgender"; Valentine (2007) *Imagining Transgender: An Ethnography of a Category*; Garrison (2018) "On the Limits of 'Trans Enough': Authenticating Trans Identity Narratives"; Johnson (2015) "Normative Accountability: How the Medical Model Influences Transgender Identities and Experiences"; Namaste (2000) "Invisible Lives: The Erasure of Transsexual and Transgendered People"; Roen (2002) "'Either/Or' and 'Both/Neither': Discursive Tensions in Transgender Politics." For origins on contemporary uses of "transgender" see Feinberg (1996) *Transgender Warriors: Making History from Joan of Arc to Dennis Rodman*; Stryker (1998) "The Transgender Issue: An Introduction."

7. Cisgender and Transgender are not nearly as mutually exclusive as people seem to think, however, as I analyze in more depth in Darwin (2020) "Challenging the Cisgender/Transgender Binary: Nonbinary People and the Transgender Label.

8. Darwin (2020) "Challenging the Cisgender/Transgender Binary: Nonbinary People and the Transgender Label."

9. Harrison-Quintana et al. (2015), Harrison et al. (2012), and Factor and Rothblum (2008).

10. Kessler and McKenna (1985).

11. Johnson, Austin H. "Normative Accountability: How the Medical Model Influences Transgender Identities and Experiences." *Sociology Compass* 9, no. 9 (2015): 803–813.

12. Shuster (2019).

13. Raewyn Connell (2009) and Carla Pfeffer (2014) have been advancing recognition/misrecognition as a sociological alternative to the "passing" paradigm. While "passing" implies that some have an authentic identity while others engage in mere mimicry, recognition/misrecognition centers the role of other social actors.

14. Bradley, Evan D., Julia Salkind, Ally Moore, and Sofi Teitsort. "Singular 'They' and Novel Pronouns: Gender-Neutral, Nonbinary, or Both?" *Proceedings of the Linguistic Society of America* 4, no. 1 (2019): 36–41.

15. Since I began publishing this research, others have begun to publish on nonbinary gender as well. Noteworthy contributions have been made by Barbee and Schrock (2019), Garrison (2018), Risman (2018), Rogers (2018), shuster (2017).

16. Harrison-Quintana et al. (2015), Harrison et al. (2012), Factor and Rothblum (2008), and Kuper et al. (2012).

17. Alexander (2002), Ashford (2009), and Campbell (2004).

18. Goffman, Erving. *The Presentation of Self in Everyday Life*. London: Harmondsworth, 1978.

19. Hillier and Harrison (2007) and Smith et al. (2015).

20. Darwin (2017).

21. Faugier and Sargeant (1997).

22. Watters and Biernacki (1989).

23. Charmaz (2006).

24. Charmaz (2006).

Reconsidering the "Gender Revolution"

I was startled to see the headline "Gender Revolution: The Shifting Land-scape of Gender" on a special issue of *National Geographic*[1] in my doctor's office in 2017. The front cover features a group of seven young adults, of varying races and gender expressions. In white print, each individual gets a gender label, including "intersex nonbinary," "transgender female," "bi-gender," "transgender male," "androgynous," and "male." In retrospect, it is clear that this special issue marked a major milestone in media representation of gender diversity. Slowly but surely, celebrities began to "come out" along the gender axis and more and more television shows began to feature gender-diverse character arcs. Then in 2019, *Merriam-Webster Dictionary*[2] declared the singular pronoun "they/them/their" the word of the year. Quite suddenly, the cultural spotlight swiveled to focus squarely on nonbinary people, who identify as neither simply "men" nor "women," but as something else entirely. Mass media finally acknowledged and validated what many of us already knew: gender diversity is very real and here to stay.

This is not to say that gender diversity itself is a new phenomenon. Across cultures and historical eras, people have more or less openly identified with a variety of genders.[3] But until this sudden explosion of celebratory media coverage, our society allowed cisgender people to pretend that no other genders exist besides man and woman. This cultural shift marks the begin-ning of an official gender expansion, or what sociologists call the "redoing" of gender, that will hopefully allow greater gender diversity to proliferate. The purpose of this book is to demystify the meaning and experience of nonbinary

© The Author(s), under exclusive license to Springer Nature
Switzerland AG 2022
H. Darwin, *Redoing Gender*,
https://doi.org/10.1007/978-3-030-83617-7_2

gender and highlight the considerable everyday labor that nonbinary people perform in order to be and "do" their gender. For while the media capitalizes upon gender diversity as a glitzy phenomenon, it simultaneously (and perhaps inadvertently) obscures the unglamorous labor that gender-diverse people have performed "backstage" to get us to this point; yet it is precisely this labor of gender outness that forces cisgender people to reconsider gender as we know it and make room for other genders in our ideologies, relationships, and social structures. This interactional labor that I call "managing gender difference" is key to understanding how this "gender revolution" came to be.

Doing and Redoing Gender

The title of this book, *Redoing Gender*, references a famous sociological concept called "doing gender," which was revolutionary for its time.[4] In the 1960s and 1970s, feminist scholars began to push back against the notion that biology is destiny, since that type of reasoning justified women's oppression under men. According to the feminist argument, biological features called "sex" may be inevitable, but gender is far from it; rather, gender is taught to people from birth.[5] As Simone de Beauvoir famously wrote, "One is not born, but rather becomes a woman."[6] Indeed, children with vaginas are taught to behave "like a lady" and children with penises are told to "man up" when they cry. Gender is socially conditioned through these repeated interactions and demonstrated through corresponding behaviors and practices. Therefore, Candace West and Don Zimmerman (1987) argued that people do not *possess* gender, so much as they *do* gender. When people "do gender" wrong, in a way that challenges the status quo, they encounter "gender-policing" responses like those mentioned above. These types of regulatory interactions represent what West and Zimmerman called "systems of accountability." People are held accountable to society's gendered norms and ideals by other people, by institutions, and even by themselves.

"Doing gender" has inspired an abundance of research into the maintenance of normative gender ideals and practices. As of this writing, the article has been cited 13,830 times (Google Scholar). Scholars have analyzed how people "do gender" through language,[7] housework,[8] crime,[9] work,[10] relationships,[11] health,[12] consumption,[13] sexuality,[14] emotions,[15] athletics,[16] and more. Reflecting the influence of intersectionality, this expansive corpus has further demonstrated that people "do gender" differently depending upon a number of factors such as race,[17] sexuality,[18] class,[19] religion,[20] and disability.[21]

The breadth of this "doing gender" corpus can be overwhelming. Sometimes it seems like it has reached saturation, leaving nothing more to write about through this lens. And yet, this expansive corpus remains primarily focused on how cisgender people "do" gender. In fact, J Sumerau and associates (2016) argue that it would be more appropriate to call this corpus "doing *cis*gender."[22] The fact that the "cis" prefix is omitted at all illustrates a process that Sumerau et al. (2016) call the "cisgendering of reality,"[23] loosely defined as the erasure of trans (and nonbinary) existence. This is an issue within the social sciences because the experiences of the gender majority (cisgender people) do not represent the experiences of gender minorities. Quite simply, gender minorities have a different experience of the systems of accountability that maintain society's gender status quo.

Some argue that the best way to understand how these systems of accountability operate is to center queer social actors, since they are the most negatively impacted by them.[24] Notionally, cisgender people take for granted the ways in which our binary-gendered society caters toward us. Queer people, by contrast, are forcefully made aware of the binary gender system's contours in day-to-day life due to their deviance from it. Indeed, this very logic accounts for West and Zimmerman's (1987) use of Garfinkel's (1967) case study of a trans woman named Agnes within their original theoretical model. And yet, the centrality of transgender (and queer) experiences within the "doing gender" corpus has waned dramatically through the years. In response to this phenomenon, Carla Pfeffer (2014) encourages sociologists of gender to re-center queer social actors. In her words: "The experiences of queer social actors hold the potential to rattle the very foundations upon which normative binaries rest, highlighting the increasingly blurry intersections, tensions, and overlaps between sex, gender, and sexual orientation in the twenty-first century."[25] This study builds upon Pfeffer's injunction by centering one such understudied queer demographic that lives life squarely within these "blurry intersections, tensions, and overlaps between sex, gender, and sexual orientation": gender nonbinary people.

Some argue that nonbinary people are transgender by default.[26] Following this logic, the sizeable transgender studies corpus should apply to nonbinary people's experiences as well. However, this conclusion would be (and is) overly simplistic. It is true that transgender people and the transgender category have captured the academic imagination for decades. As David Valentine (2007) argued in *Imagining Transgender*, transgender has become a "central cultural site where meanings about gender and sexuality are being worked out."[27]

Unfortunately, our empirical knowledge about the transgender community is limited by systematic measurement errors in censuses and other surveys. For example, we tend to ask people whether they are cisgender *or* transgender—a false binary that excludes many nonbinary people who feel uncomfortable with both categories.[28] The relationship between transgender people and the gender binary system is in actuality quite diverse[29]: some abide by society's gender ideals and pursue a relatively binary gender transition while others make a point to self-consciously "rebel" against binary gender norms.[30]

When people refuse to "do" their gender the way that society expects them to, they effectively contribute toward a process that West and Zimmerman (2009) call the "redoing" of gender. Gender is not necessarily "undone"[31] in these moments, as some have argued, so much as it is revised (or "redone") according to an adjusted set of rules and criteria. Indeed, systems of accountability still exist even when society becomes more progressive, as this book will make abundantly clear. Any time nonbinary people experience discrimination, harassment, or more casual forms of "gender-policing" in this book, we will see evidence of these lingering systems of accountability. Similarly, any time nonbinary people succeed in "doing" their gender in a nonconventional way without incurring harassment, and/or manage to assert themselves as nonbinary, we will see evidence of shifting and relaxing norms of social acceptability.

This shift, or the "redoing of gender," is the central interest of this book. The so-called gender revolution heralded by *National Geographic* is really just a formal acknowledgment that the rules of gender have changed. Gender is not as simple as people used to believe and may still want to believe. But what *is* new is society's recognition of gender diversity as legitimate. This is a historical moment for our culture and one that warrants closer analysis. This book helps us understand this social change process by showing the labor that goes into it, the "social mechanisms" that facilitate this expansion. Changing the rules is hard to do. Those who love the old rules are wont to protect them with great vehemence against any and all who would threaten them. It is scary, draining, emotional work and it falls largely upon the people who are marginalized and in the greatest danger. Nonbinary people are on the frontlines of this gender revolution, whether they like it or not, since their very existence is political.

Coming Out as Nonbinary

Because the sociological study of nonbinary gender is just beginning, many questions remain unanswered. Is there a nonbinary gender? Is nonbinary gender an identity? What are the obstacles that nonbinary people encounter while trying to assert their existence? How do nonbinary people achieve their gender in a society that denies and erases their existence? In sexuality studies, this type of interactional work is oftentimes conceptualized as "coming out." But what does the "coming out" process look like for nonbinary people, who have been rendered unintelligible—that is, incomprehensible—within the binary gender system? Is this interactive process different from gay and lesbian people's experiences in any sort of significant way? After all, "coming out" has been theorized at length within psychological sexuality studies[32] and sociological sexuality studies.[33] And yet, this corpus remains predominantly concerned with the experiences of sexual minorities. The particularities of *gender* minorities' "coming out" experiences remain undertheorized and underexplored.

The exception to this rule is a very small body of research on transgender coming out experiences. Based on previous studies as well as their own data collection, Brumbaugh-Johnson et al. (2019) conclude:

> Scholars should conceptualize transgender coming out as an ongoing social process, not only because transgender individuals must make decisions about identity disclosure every time they meet a new person, but also because coming out involves a constant navigation of the social implications of having a gender identity that is not well accepted.[34]

Brumbaugh-Johnson et al. (2019) argue that the transgender "coming out" experience should be understood as a lifelong "career,"[35] as opposed to a discreet one-time event. Meanwhile, they carefully acknowledge the limited applicability of their findings to nonbinary and genderqueer populations, since their research selectively focused on people who identify with the transgender label and disproportionately featured trans men and trans women as a result. This book builds upon Brumbaugh-Johnson et al.'s (2019) findings by highlighting particularities of gender nonbinary identity management techniques. My interviewees are not simply "navigat[ing] the social implications of having a gender identity that is not well accepted"; rather, they are navigating the practical implications of having a gender identity that people have never even heard of before.

The demands of the "coming out career" for nonbinary people extend far beyond a simple declarative statement. Nonbinary people must also brace themselves to contend with people's reactions to their disclosure, including hurtful exchanges that question and delegitimize their identity.[36] A parallel can be found in literature on the bisexuality stigma, as bi+ people also contend with accusations that their identity is not real, that they must pick one of the two binary options (straight or gay), or that they are simply confused and transitioning to one or the other binary categories.[37] However, the crucial distinction remains, that the public has at least heard of bisexuality before this hypothetical exchange.

The case of nonbinary gender outness also differs from the sexuality context because a nonbinary gender disclosure often goes hand in hand with a request that others shift to gender-neutral terminology when referring to them thereafter.[38] As this type of linguistic shift deviates from habit, it requires significant effort from others, especially from those who have never heard of nonbinary gender before this disclosure. This request for linguistic recognition renders the nonbinary person profoundly vulnerable to rejection, misrecognition, and delegitimizing interactions following the disclosure.[39]

Between the near-constant misgendering in daily life and the public's lack of awareness (and/or acceptance) that nonbinary gender exists, the "coming out" career of nonbinary people is exhausting. This book will demonstrate that nonbinary people are thus prone to the phenomenon that sociologists have studied in other people-oriented careers called "burnout."[40] Nonbinary people must carefully manage their emotions and exhaustion while managing their stigmatized identities throughout their lifelong "coming out" careers. This is an interactive process that I call "managing gender difference." As the rest of this book illustrates, "managing gender difference" *can* contribute toward social change, but it doesn't always—sometimes exhaustion management concerns are more pressing than the need to be recognized.

Chapter Summaries

The structure of this book has arisen organically out of the "doing gender" model. Again, according to the model, there are three levels of "accountability." (1) People hold *themselves* accountable to gender ideals that they have internalized; (2) people hold *one another* accountable to gender norms, and (3) *institutions* hold people accountable to the gender status quo by selectively recognizing the legitimacy of certain categories. I analyze how nonbinary people push back against each of these three levels of accountability in separate chapters—however, I distribute the interpersonal level across two chapters, so as to separately explore how people signify their gender to strangers and how they "redo relationships" with loved ones. At each of these levels of accountability, I will demonstrate that nonbinary people invest a significant amount of labor into expanding the range of viable ways of "doing gender."

Rethinking Sex and Gender

I begin this analysis at the most micro and intimate level. After all, before nonbinary people can begin to advocate for themselves and announce their presence, they need to realize that they *are* nonbinary. This realization often occurs later than sexuality realizations for the people in my sample, because they simply do not know that their gendered discomfort is valid, has a name, and that others feel the same way. To get to this epiphany, people have to go through a laborious and often painful stage of "identity work"[41] that I call "rethinking" sex and gender. They must realize that their genitals do not dictate their gender and that their gender is not a good fit in any of the well-advertised gender categories. One of my interviewees describes this process as going through a type of flowchart, trying out different labels and identities until they finally find the one that fits. This chapter illustrates this process, while introducing the reader to the nuances and identity politics wrapped up in the various labels under discussion. Along the way, the reader will get to know some of the people who shared their stories for this book.

Resignifying Gender

After realizing that they are nonbinary, most of the people in this sample altered the way that they verbally and visually present themselves to the world. While some insist that they do this purely for themselves, in order to feel more like their gender, others are self-consciously attempting to minimize misgendering through their new visual cues. This resignification process includes changes to wardrobe, head hair, body hair, facial hair, and chests. Some also announce alternative pronouns to people when they meet them, in an effort to verbally signify their gender, or they assert their proper pronoun as soon as they experience verbal misgendering. Many others silently permit misgendering out of a sense of self-preservation. As this chapter will emphasize, the risks and benefits of this decision are varied and complicated. Sometimes it is dangerous to achieve recognition as nonbinary, such as while using public restrooms.

Redoing Relationships

It can also be difficult to achieve gender recognition in relationships. Parents, siblings, friends, and lovers are accustomed to interacting with people in a certain manner. Sociologists refer to this interactional phenomenon as relationship "scripts."[42] There are different scripts for how to interact with one's daughter vs. one's son; one's sister vs. one's brother; one's boyfriend vs. one's girlfriend, etc.; however, all of these scripts are structured around the gender binary. Therefore, after a nonbinary person announces their gender to their loved ones, these scripts need to change. Nonbinary people need their loved ones to participate in a veritable "redoing" of the relationship. These relational shifts are rarely quick or easy. Rather, nonbinary people often invest a significant amount of labor into helping these shifts happen, by providing explanations, coaching the person through proper protocol, reminding them whenever they slip up, and enduring whatever emotions the other person must process in order to get on board with the change. Out of anticipatory exhaustion, some permit misgendering to continue in select relationships. The alternative simply requires a prohibitively massive investment of their time and energy.

Resisting Erasure

Even if people manage to get their loved ones to acknowledge their gender as nonbinary, they still contend with misgendering from institutions. On surveys, forms, and official identification documents, nonbinary people are routinely coerced into misgendering themselves through mandatory questions about their gender. I call this the "binary box dilemma." Sometimes the question asks for sex, but oftentimes it asks about gender, before providing binary options "male" and "female" as synonymous with "man" and "woman." The ramifications of this question are profound, since universities, workplaces, and medical systems defer to legal documentation about the person's identity. This chapter explores the ways in which nonbinary people have fought this institutional erasure of gender diversity, if and when they have been able to respond to it. However, it must be noted that they are usually not even given the chance to fight back.

Regression and Progress

I finish this book by offering the reader a glimpse into the lives of my interviewees four years later. Do they think it has gotten any easier to achieve recognition as nonbinary in society? Do they assert themselves more than they used to, or perhaps less? Has their self-presentation style or pronoun practice changed over time? Moreover, do they even still identify as nonbinary? This follow-up addresses the assumption that nonbinary gender is just a phase while offering insight into whether progressive social change has marched forward along a continuum—or not so much.

Conclusion

Through identity work, relational work, and bureaucratic work, nonbinary people invest considerable labor into achieving social recognition. This fight can be dangerous for some and prohibitively exhausting for others; as a result, many people in my sample begrudgingly accept misgendering from strangers and casual associates. Nonbinary people do not announce their presence or achieve social recognition nearly as often as they would like to in an ideal world.

It would be much easier for nonbinary people to achieve social recognition if the general public was familiar with the notion of gender diversity; however, this shift is slow to effect when the relatively small demographics of nonbinary and transgender people are tasked with placing themselves in danger and assuming all of the educational labor. One of my purposes in writing this book is to share the "explanatory burden" that oftentimes falls upon the shoulders of this already over-taxed population. Cisgender allies must become more vocal and more active in educating other cisgender people about gender diversity. I conclude this book by expanding upon J Orne's notion of "ally consciousness,"[43] as it is experienced by nonbinary people. Interviewees voice gratitude for friends and partners who correct people when they misgender them and thereby spare them the discomfort and fear that accompanies such omnipresent corrective labor. Although an expansion of socially viable gender categories is underway, it is clear that this shift hasn't happened without a fight. Nonbinary people shouldn't have to fight this battle against the binary gender system alone. Everyone will benefit when the rules of gender relax.

Notes

1. Gender Revolution, Gender. "National Geographic." *Single Issue* (2017).
2. "Merriam-Webster's Words of the Year 2019." https://www.merriam-webster. com/words-at-play/word-of-the-year.
3. Stryker, Susan, and Paisley Currah. "General Editors' Introduction." *Transgender Studies Quarterly* 1, no. 3 (2014): 303–307.
4. West and Zimmerman (1987).
5. Kessler and McKenna (1985).
6. Simone de Beauvoir, *The Second Sex.*
7. Coates (2015) and Bucholtz and Hall (2005).
8. Bianchi et al. (2000), Brines (1994), Bittman et al. (2003), and Shelton and John (1996).
9. Messerschmidt (2007), Richie (2018), Messerschmidt (2019), and Heimer and Coster (1999).
10. McDowell (2011), Correll (2001), Ridgeway (1997), Williams (1995), Martin (2002), Bruni et al. (2004).
11. Bird (1996), Ridgeway (2009), Leidner (1991), and Pascoe (2005).
12. O'brien et al. (2005).
13. Johnston and Baumann (2014).
14. Connell (1992).
15. Bolton (2004).
16. Anderson (2010).
17. Hill (2002), Pyke and Johnson (2003), and Fenstermaker and West (2013).
18. Schilt and Westbrook (2009), Trautner (2005), Vidal-Ortiz (2005).
19. Trautner (2005) and Acker (2006).
20. Avishai (2008), Darwin (2018), Irby (2014), and Rao (2015).
21. Ahlsen et al. (2014).
22. Sumerau and Mathers (2019).
23. Sumerau et al. (2016).
24. Vidal-Ortiz (2009) and Pfeffer (2014).
25. Pfeffer (2014, 10).
26. Darwin (2020).
27. Valentine (2007, 14).
28. Darwin (2020), Westbrook and Saperstein (2015), and Sumerau et al. (2017).
29. See Schilt and Lagos (2017).
30. See Risman (2019).
31. Butler (2004), Deutsch (2007), Risman (2009).
32. Cass (1979, 1984), Coleman (1982), Troiden (1989), Rust (1993), Oswald (2000), and Saltzburg (2004).
33. Horowitz and Newcomb (2002), Kaufman and Johnson (2004), Glover et al. (2009), Wolkomir (2009).
34. Brumbaugh-Johnson et al. (2019, 1171).

35. Guittar and Rayburn (2016) have argued elsewhere that "coming out" should be understood as a lifelong career, in recognition of the ongoing and oftentimes lifelong identity management considerations it entails.
36. See Shuster (2017).
37. Eisner (2013) and Sumerau et al. (2019).
38. Darwin (2017).
39. Shuster (2017).
40. Maslach (1981).
41. Snow and Anderson (1987).
42. See the extensive works of John H. Gagnon and William Simon on "sexual scripts".
43. Orne (2013).

Rethinking Sex and Gender

"The way I think genderqueer identification for me ended up rolling out, it's like, you're gay, but not exactly. Like, I'm a boy, but not exactly. Or I'm a tomboy, but not exactly. So, you're just going through this little…almost like a flowchart" River explained to me. River, a 34-year-old white Jewish person from New York City, discovered their genderqueer identity later in life than my college-aged interviewees. But, they knew that something was different about their gender for some time before arriving at that label.

River's flowchart metaphor makes one thing clear: before anyone can start to "redo" gender at the interactional or institutional level, they have to first rethink it. For nonbinary people, this "rethinking" process is extremely intimate, complicated, and intertwined with their evolving understanding of their sexuality. Nonbinary people are told at birth that their assigned sex equates to a corresponding binary gender. Doctors in the delivery room proclaim "It's a boy!" upon detecting a penis or "It's a girl!" upon detecting a vagina. Problematically, sex is not reducible to outward appearances of genitalia, nor are the differences between penises and vaginas nearly so binary as the medical establishment would have us imagine—but that is beyond the scope of this book.[1]

Thus, people are born with not just an assigned binary sex, but an assigned binary gender as well. It takes time for people to realize that sex does not necessarily determine gender and to further discover that there are other gender categories beyond the binary parameters of man/woman or trans man/trans woman. It takes time for gay, lesbian, and queer people to realize

H. Darwin, *Redoing Gender*,
https://doi.org/10.1007/978-3-030-83617-7_3

that their gender discomfort is not necessarily a byproduct of their sexuality, but rather attributable to gender dysphoria. It takes time for people to "come out" as nonbinary if they have already "come out" as gay/lesbian/trans woman/trans man—as though there is a set quota on how many times a person is allowed to "come out." I analyze this internal process as "identity work."[2]

I began my interviews by asking people to explain why they replied to my call for respondents—what about the terms that I used applies to them? Are they nonbinary? Genderqueer? Do they also identify as transgender? Why or why not? And what is it about the categories "woman" and "man" that doesn't resonate with them? The purpose of this chapter is to introduce the reader to the complexities of gender "identity work," while highlighting the nuances between different labels, ways of identifying, and conceptualizations of gender within this sample. For cisgender readers, this chapter will help you understand key terms used throughout the rest of this book. I hope you will come away with an appreciation for the amount of labor that people have already invested into discovering that they are nonbinary before they "come out" to others. For trans, nonbinary, and gender-questioning readers, this chapter will lend insight into the inner-most processes of some nonbinary people's "identity work," illuminating similarities and differences between your own experience of gender and those of the people in this sample.

I structure this chapter in keeping with River's flowchart concept, highlighting the trial and error process that ultimately leads many people to realize that they are nonbinary. While some feel as though they were "born this way," others cite concrete catalysts that helped them realize they were nonbinary. Not everyone claims to have always known—instead, the discovery of terminology was pivotal to many people's "gender journeys." This chapter concludes by explaining what transgender, genderqueer, and nonbinary mean to my interviewees, as well as what pronouns they use and why.

Born This Way?

Few of my interviewees claim to have always known that they were nonbinary. Rather, there was something about the gender category that they were forced into at birth that simply never felt quite right. They felt a constant low-grade gender discomfort. "I was never that sort of 'classic case' of gender non-conformity that they were used to, of the narrative of being born in the wrong body. That was never a thing," explained Corey, a white 28-year-old Jewish interviewee. At the time of this interview, Corey had just started to see the effects of their testosterone hormone therapy. Their voice was getting lower and their facial hair and body hair was thicker and more noticeable. They were pleased with these changes, but remained disinterested in "passing" as a man. As with Corey, most of the people I interviewed report always feeling vaguely uncomfortable in both binary gender categories. Hunter, a nineteen-year-old mixed-race college student put it concisely when they explained, "My entire life I never felt fully female but I also never felt fully male."

The majority of my interviewees cite specific people, college courses, communities, or Internet forums that helped them realize that they were nonbinary later in life. I call these "catalysts of awakening." Indeed, the rise of the Internet has been widely linked to the rise of the Transgender Rights movement, as this platform enabled marginalized and geographically disparate people to find one another and share their common experiences. Hayden, a white 21-year-old undergraduate student, directly attributes Internet access to their gender awakening: "I was raised extremely conservatively. Then I ended up getting a Tumblr when I was 16 and I found out all this interesting information and I was like, 'Oh! I didn't know people actually did that. That sounds like something I want to do!'" Carter, a white 20-year-old undergraduate student shared a similar story: "I think the first breakthrough I really made was when I was watching a YouTube video of a trans woman talking about her experiences and the thing is that I didn't really feel like I related to her experiences. I didn't really feel a connection to the female gender. But I had this weird feeling of, like, I didn't fit in either the male category or the female category."

A few people discovered that nonbinary was a valid gender option in college, during Gender Studies courses. For example, Adrian, a white 26-year-old government employee shared, "It was when I was taking my feminist theories class at the college that I went to in 2009, 2010. Talking to my friends about gender, figuring out that I didn't actually have to identify as a woman if I didn't want to, and that was the realization that changed my life." Peyton, a white 29-year-old graduate student had a similar experience: "When I was a teenager I didn't really have words for it I just had like a sense. It wasn't until I got into my undergraduate years and started reading like queer theory and queer scholarship that I began to understand that there was a term for it."

Some discovered that they were nonbinary when they finally gained access to gender-diverse groups of people. As white 29-year-old Carson explained, "When I got to Uni, I started getting involved with queer groups and I started meeting people who identified as genderqueer—around 19, 20, 21. That was when I really started to realize that there was another option. That you could exist outside of the binary and when that was explained to me it was like the lightbulb went off: 'This is how I've been feeling my whole life!'" (Lest readers come away mistakenly thinking that college turns people nonbinary, I should emphasize here that Carson was *always* nonbinary. Their college experiences simply validated their experiences and introduced them to the gender label as well as its corresponding community.) And finally, for Rowan, a mixed-race 22-year old, the mere distance from home that college afforded proved instrumental to their ability to finally explore their gender: "As a kid you grow up with these ideas of what you're supposed to be, and how you're supposed to act, and that never sat right with me. It wasn't until I left my home town and was in college that I realized, 'I don't think that I'm a woman.' And the first time that I voiced that, it felt really good."

Clearly, some nonbinary people do maintain that they were "born this way," never comfortable in the gender category that was assigned to them at birth. However, they only self-consciously became "nonbinary" when they discovered that label later in life. Peyton explains: "As I got older and as terminology has become—and identity has become—much more available, I realized, like, 'No, there's actually words for this, and I fit in to a larger category. It's just not the categories I was raised with'" (Peyton). Corey elaborates upon this same generational experience: "I think I definitely needed words that I didn't have back then. I needed vocabulary that didn't exist in 2008 to explain my gender identity. If I had had the words, I probably would have come out as nonbinary then." The relatively recent proliferation of identity terminology, coupled with its increasing accessibility and visibility, has helped Peyton and Corey understand themselves much better. This access to language and the contingent sense of validation—that what they were experiencing was real and not just in their head—was missing for most of my interviewees for much of their lives. It was much easier for them to learn about and identify as gay, lesbian, and/or transgender. The following sections will elaborate.

Gay?

The vast majority of LGBQ people in my sample "came out" as gay, lesbian, or queer long before "coming out" as nonbinary. Most people used one or more of the following sexuality labels: queer ($n = 19$), gay ($n = 8$), bisexual ($n = 7$), pansexual ($n = 6$), androsexual ($n = 3$), asexual ($n = 3$), straight ($n = 2$), gynesexual ($n = 2$), nonbinary lesbian ($n = 2$), gynephilic ($n = 1$), panromantic ($n = 1$), demisexual ($n = 1$), and graysexual ($n = 1$).[3] Many mistakenly assumed that their sexual identity accounted for their gender discomfort, a conclusion which stalled their gender exploration for many years. In Dubbs' (32-year-old, white) words: "Growing up, I thought that all of the discomfort and issues and things that I felt had to do with my sexuality not my gender identity." Parker, a 29-year-old Filipinx graduate student, shared a similar experience:

> I got teased a lot as a child for being you know like a fairy or gay or, you know, all the nice things that children say to each other. But I never really thought that had anything to do with my gender because until maybe mid-college, gender and sex were the same to me. I was male—therefore my gender was male.

This conflation between sex, gender, and sexuality has led to the cultural stereotype that lesbians are manly and gay men are feminine, known in academic circles as the sexual-inversion stigma.[4] Within this cultural context, cisgender people (alleged "gender normals")[5] assume that gender non-conforming peers are simply gay or lesbian, rather than nonbinary. In turn, nonbinary people are exposed to this logic—and oftentimes internalize its conclusion. Justice, a 26-year-old Latinx/Native American with a lesbian mother, received these messages rather abruptly when they moved from the Czech Republic to the United States as a teenager: "Like, I got called a dyke and faggot and stuff and I was like, 'Ok great, I guess that's what I am. I guess I'm a dyke, I guess I'm a lesbian.'" Yet, even after coming out as lesbian, something still didn't feel quite right about their gender as "woman."

Reagan, a white 32-year old, shared a vivid memory of the moment when they realized that they weren't a lesbian:

> I always knew I was gay, from the first moment I was able to recognize thoughts or things. But always somehow knew that it was wrong, and so never ever talked about it with anyone. So that means that I was, like, really depressed and really anxious, and drank a lot, and smoked pot a lot and tried to hide and drown—basically drown out all those feelings. And then when I got to 20 I came out and kind of thought that all of that anxiety and depression would disappear once I was true to myself. And it didn't. But it also didn't occur to me that there could also be something else going on beneath the surface, so…It wasn't until I was I guess maybe 29–I'm 32 now…I was at this lipstick lesbian awareness party, and felt really out of place…even though at that time I identified as a lesbian—because women identify as lesbian and I was gay, so… it just, like, these words are where I'm getting caught up in my identity. And so, I was like, "Well, I'm definitely a lesbian, but I don't identify as a femme.

But I still feel really out of place in this all-women space." And it kind of hit me in that moment of like…"Wait a second. I'm not a lesbian because I don't identify with 'woman.'" And so, from there was a lot of exploring "So what does that mean? How do I identify?" And I, you know, went into therapy and went to therapy twice a week and was trying to really figure out what was going on for me.

As Reagan recounted this memory, their voice filled with emotion. Part of Reagan's distress derived from their longing for membership in an identity group that would feel like home. They thought they were going to achieve that feeling when they came out as lesbian, but in order to be a part of the lesbian community, they had to suppress and deny their discomfort in the woman category. At a certain point, this price became unbearably high. The prospect of having to find a new home and go through the coming out process all over again was overwhelming for them, but they simply couldn't put it off any longer. They were "drowning."

Lisa's experience is another one that highlights how the sexual inversion stigma can delay people's gender journeys. Lisa is admittedly a bit of an outlier in this sample of nonbinary people, but her experience helpfully illustrates that people can discover their nonbinary gender identity at any phase of life—not just when they are young. Lisa is a 60-year-old white interfaith minister who was first (mistakenly) introduced to me as a drag queen. Indeed, Lisa's self-presentation seemed very much in alignment with the drag queen label. Well over six feet tall and muscular with a strong jaw, Lisa was resplendent in bold stage makeup, a well-coiffed blonde wig, and flowing jewel toned garments, accompanied by high heels. However, when I spoke with her after the service about this research project, she excitedly disclosed that she is genderqueer and would happily grant me an interview. I was a little surprised that when I next saw Lisa over Skype, she was dressed very differently. Settled in for a lazy day at home, she wore a black T-shirt, no makeup, and no wig. She had short-cropped dark brown hair, tan skin, and kind brown eyes.

Lisa enthusiastically explained to me that she identified as a gay man for many decades before realizing that there was something else going on. She encountered her first "catalyst of awakening" when she was in her thirties and joined the Radical Fairy commune in Vermont, a collective that is famous for its unapologetic gay flamboyance. Recalling that era, Lisa mused, "I really felt like I found my tribe. I felt like I found an explanation for who I was—like, finally!" At the commune, it was commonplace for members to play with gender and don feminine personas and appearances. There, Lisa acquired her name and developed a stage persona that she brought back with her to New York City a decade later. However, once in New York, Lisa began to have an identity crisis and became desperate to bring her male body into alignment with her assigned gender. In order to feel more like a man, she took testosterone supplements, exercised rigorously, and engaged in promiscuity. During this time, she also enrolled in seminary and met the man whom she eventually married. This period of life proved to be pivotal to her gender journey: by the end of her time at seminary, Lisa had reembraced her feminine side, making peace with it as a gift from God.

Although Lisa is unique in many ways, her story also highlights some common themes among my interviews. Lisa first "came out" along the sexuality axis, under the assumption that she was the sex/gender assigned to her at birth. Only later, after living in this identity for a while, did she realize that it didn't quite fit and that there was something different about her gender as well. At this point, it was incumbent upon her to explore her gender, express it, and "come out" as nonbinary to her loved ones—in this case, her husband. A related question that Lisa asked herself during this time was whether she was "born in the wrong body" and in fact a woman. This internally posed question was the last step before discovering nonbinary for most people in my sample as they traveled through the veritable identity flowchart.

Transgender?

This process of rethinking sex and gender, that leads the people in this sample to identify as nonbinary or genderqueer, does not necessarily lead all of them to also identify with the transgender label. Most people who I interviewed do identify to some extent with the transgender label, but responses were split between those who unequivocally affirmed their identification ($n = 14$) and those who voiced considerably more ambivalence ($n = 23$). Lisa identifies as transgender, but she prefers to think of "trans" as an abbreviation for "transcendent." Reagan used to identify as transgender, but doesn't anymore. Parker identifies as nonbinary, but maintains that they are not "trans enough" to qualify for transgender group membership.[6] Although nonbinary is oftentimes presented to the public and to the academy as a straightforward subcategory of transgender, it is clear that this way of thinking about it is overly simplistic. Nonbinary is best understood as a gender category unto itself that sometimes—but not always—overlaps with transgender.

Not Transgender

But first, it is important to emphasize that ten of my interviewees do *not* identify as transgender. Avery is a tall, thin, white graduate student with sandy blonde hair styled asymmetrically, shaved close on one side with long side-swept bangs. A long-time member of the gay community, Avery has only recently begun to tell people about their nonbinary gender. When I asked if they identify as transgender, Avery quickly said no. They then elaborated:

> I don't view myself on the level of Caitlyn Jenner or the level of my friends who are "dressing for the part" consistently... doing it in every capacity of your daily life, which I know so many of my trans friends do. Inside the house, outside the house, in the club, on streets, on public transport, wherever. In their jobs...they dress to their gender identity and express that they are female-identified.

Avery's concerns about "dressing the part" and trans legitimacy were shared by two others who were assigned male at birth as well. Mason, a 28-year-old Asian-American graduate student, invoked the same logic, while clarifying that once they can afford a new feminine wardrobe, they will begin to feel more comfortable claiming the transgender label. For this contingent, rethinking sex and gender is not enough; one has to visually and interactively engage in the redoing of gender as well, in order to qualify as transgender.

Beyond wardrobe transitions, some believe that they would have to physically transition through hormones or surgery to the "other" binary gender, in order to qualify as transgender. This type of response generally invokes the understanding of transgender as synonymous with transsexual, and the corresponding belief that all transgender people are necessarily trans women or trans men. As Mason explains: "I don't know if I feel quite comfortable sort of calling myself transgender, at least at this point, because I'm not interested in sort of fully transitioning all the way to female. And I'm not on HRT quite yet." Mason is not alone in espousing this logic, as Rhiannon (white, 24) echoes Mason's concerns:

> I don't wanna be on T, on testosterone, or anything like that. And I don't want top surgery or anything like that. So, I would feel weird calling myself transgender when there are people who, you know, do need those things and don't have the access to them, that they should rightfully have. That go through certain problems...

Rhiannon conditions the claim to a transgender identity upon a certain type of struggle that they imagine "real" transgender people experience while navigating medicalized transitions. Because they have not experienced this particular set of challenges, they do not believe that they have earned the transgender label. Mason and Rhiannon have internalized the transgender binary's sex/gender conflation even though they have disentangled their own gender from the sex assigned to them at birth.

Parker also believes that they have not experienced sufficient hardship to lay claim to the transgender label; however, they understand social discrimination, instead of medical transitioning, to be the central experiential criterion for trans inclusion:

> I do not consider myself as transgender. I feel like they go through… they have a much harder time with their identities than I do with society. So, they get way more push back because people have a really hard time accepting that somebody who looks male or looks female identifies as the opposite. Or that somebody would want to even undergo surgery—or something like that—to actually transform their body to match their identity. People have a really hard time with that. And with mine, it's just like a "Well, you're just being difficult," you know. Or like, "Ok, well, I'll just ignore it" kind of thing. It's like my identity is much easier for society to ignore than somebody who is trans.

Parker conditions their disidentification from the transgender label upon an imagined oppression hierarchy. Parker likes to wear bright colors and keeps their fingernails long, but otherwise presents in a way that gets misrecognized as "man." Since binary transgender people experience a more difficult time in society than they do, they do not feel comfortable using the transgender label.

On the other hand, Harley explains that she does not identify as transgender because "It's not necessarily me changing my gender. It's coming to a balance of something that I felt for a long time." Harley is a white 30-year-old dance instructor in the Bay Area who only recently came out as nonbinary after giving the matter much thought. Harley is aware that some might consider her to be transgender, but she is wary of this categorical tendency as well as the growing popularity of the transgender label more broadly: "I see some people identifying as trans and coming out as 'they' for more political reasons than actual personal reasons and I'm trying to avoid that. I'm trying to be as authentic to who I feel I am." Harley considers politically motivated identities to be disingenuous. In order to avoid becoming what she calls a "transtrender," she avoids using the pronoun "they" as well as the transgender label. And yet, while trying to remain authentic to herself, she ultimately holds herself accountable to popular (mis)understandings of transgender as well as of nonbinary gender.

To recap, there are various reasons why nonbinary people might not identify as transgender. These reasons include an internalized sense of accountability to the transgender binary, an understanding of transgender as a continuum, or an association of transgender with a particular type of suffering. For lots of reasons, these ten do not identify as transgender. Yet, they are oftentimes shepherded under the "transgender umbrella" by others, both academics and laypeople alike, by virtue of their nonbinary gender.[7]

Yes Transgender

Meanwhile, fourteen of my interviewees unequivocally answered "yes" when asked if they identify as transgender. Sequoia is a 21-year-old Argentinian undergraduate student of Latinx and Middle Eastern descent who Skyped in from Buenos Aires. They had short-cropped wavy black hair, an olive skin tone, and big earnest brown eyes. They were extremely excited to participate in this interview because they were currently thinking and talking a lot about their gender with their girlfriend who was beginning to question her own gender as well. When I asked if Sequoia identified as transgender, they provided a seemingly apolitical response, based on a presumed technicality: "Yes, if I don't consider myself a woman, then by default, if I'm not a man, then I'm transgender. So, I'm not in transition, but I'm in a constant…change. In the sense of, there's no box that you could put me in or that I feel comfortable with you putting me." Sequoia's response was echoed by a few other people as well, such as white 22-year-old Morgan who flatly replied, "I do, just because I don't identify as cis. And that's mainly it." Clearly, Sequoia and Morgan interpret the meaning of transgender differently than the people in the previous section, even though they all identify as nonbinary.

Why and how has this difference arisen and does it even matter? Carson believes that it does very much matter if nonbinary people lay claim to the transgender label, as a gesture of solidarity with those who stand out more conspicuously as gender non-normative. A white 29-year-old high school teacher in the Bay Area, Carson believes that their decision to claim the label might make the school a safer place for gender non-conforming youth:

> We had an incident out here. A kid, they were a gender non-conforming kid asleep on the bus, and some other kids set their dress on fire. This student in question was significantly injured, was recovered with second degree burns, and that was definitely a moment that I felt I needed to be more public

and out with work and make a space for my students who might be in that identification. Since then I felt more a push to be more open with coming out.

Carson very self-consciously identifies with the transgender label, with the hopes that they might leverage their influence as a teacher to improve matters for the next generation of trans and gender non-conforming people.

Others claim the transgender label in resistance against transnormativity—that is, overly simplistic generalizations about what it means to be transgender that erase transgender diversity.[8] Devin and Cleopatra are two such individuals. Cleopatra is a 23-year-old Yemenite Sephardic Jew from an ultra-Orthodox Jewish neighborhood in Brooklyn. They never exactly "came out" as nonbinary, but rather started expressing their gender non-normativity once they came out as gay at age 21. Their self-discovery process has been an extremely painful one, as their formative years in religious schools revolved around binary ideologies: "heteronormative rules around me really defined what I am." When they came out to their mother as gay, she made it clear that she expected them to continue presenting in a normative masculine fashion: "She always pressured me to be religious and to be in the closet. For a while she said 'You can't be gay.' Then she said 'Ok, you can be gay, but don't be open about it, don't wave a flag and, like, always be quiet.' Be her little religious boy that she wants, you know." One day when Cleopatra returned home after a Gay Pride parade, they discovered that their mother had locked them out of their house. After living for some time in a homeless shelter where they felt extremely unsafe, they moved in with their grandmother. Throughout all of this, Cleopatra tried to seek support from other transgender members of the Orthodox Jewish community, but without success:

> There's an Orthodox woman who is a trans woman in my neighborhood who I tried to seek support for a long time. She was part of this group for people who are formerly Orthodox or Orthodox that are trans and I looked interested in gaining support and she's like, "Oh, you're not trans," you know. Or there are people that I was speaking to on social media where the trans woman says, "Oh, you're not trans, you're just confused." I definitely hear a lot that people say that, like, "Oh, if you haven't struggled and made the choices like us, you're not trans."

Cleopatra continues to identify as trans despite these encounters with rejection and gatekeeping, but their mental health suffers in the process. By being unapologetically themselves, Cleopatra hopes to increase visibility of gender diversity and make the world an easier place for the next generation.

Devin, a 24-year-old Romani intersex activist, also contends with gate-keeping when they use the transgender label. Devin has long straight black hair, parted at the side that falls across part of their face. Their hair dramatically contrasts against their extremely fair skin. They had a quiet confidence about them when they spoke and a bit of a coy smile at times. My interview with Devin proved to be particularly valuable because they are the only intersex person in my sample. I did not know this before the interview, but Devin quickly offered up this information when I inquired into their birth assignment's impact on their gender journey:

> My birth assignment is kind of a complicated thing because I'm intersex. And I was forcibly corrected or mutilated at birth so my birth assignment was coercive. So, with regard to that, like, I don't like to disclose my binary birth assignment. It's something that was selected at random and it has a very traumatic history for me with regard to that.

When I asked if they identify with the transgender label, they emphatically assented:

> I strongly associate the trans label with kind of being open about my dysphoria and accepting it and being able to deal with it and I was able to find more supportive people in the trans community by being able to say that I'm trans. I also feel like the trans label is a very broad one and there's a lot of binary trans people and there's a lot of people who support binary trans people who don't think that nonbinary people can be trans so I like to also disperse the truth about the fact that we can be trans.

People like Devin and Cleopatra have had to rethink the meaning of transgender, while rethinking the binary sex/gender conflation itself. Some of these fourteen "yes transgender" interviewees yearn for a sense of group membership within the transgender community, but others question whether such a community even exists. Regardless of the interpersonal dynamics with which they contend, they have all internally rejected their accountability to binary gender and transgender models that erase their existence. Their identity is nonbinary and transgender, with or without others' approval.

Ambivalent

In addition to those who answered "yes" or "no" to my question about transgender identity, twenty-three responded with markedly more ambivalence. Ultimately, these twenty-three individuals fell under two broad categories:

those who consider themselves to be "under the transgender umbrella" but not "transgender" per se, and those who specify their identity specifically as "nonbinary transgender."

Some people feel strongly about qualifying their transgender identity to avoid being mistaken as trans men or trans women—or so they can safeguard themselves against slipping back into that identity. Six people in my sample previously identified as trans men or trans women because they were unaware of other options. However, after a while, they found that the same gender constraints that chafed within the binary cisgender system carried over into the binary transgender system as well. Kazi is one such individual. Kazi is a 20-year-old Bengali undergraduate student in New York with long black hair, a brown skin tone, and large dark-lashed brown eyes. When Kazi realized that they did not identify as a woman, they assumed they were a trans man by default. However, after they started their testosterone hormone regimen, they began to harbor doubts about this as well. As they recount in the following passage:

> As I started getting more comfortable with who I was, how I identified, I actually started getting more and more comfortable with the idea of feminine things…and I started getting confused. Like, "Well, I can't be a trans man if I'm comfortable with my genitals or if I don't react when people call me 'she.'" I got very confused. Like, what am I if I'm not a trans man? And I started looking it up... While I was following other trans men and other trans people's blogs, I found someone who identifies as neither. It was someone nonbinary. They didn't use "he/his" pronouns. They didn't use "she/hers." They only went by "them." And I was like, "This is really interesting." They gave me a much broader idea of what gender is, and something about that just clicked for me, you know? It's like, "That's it. That's it. That's it."

Kazi, along with many others, created a sense of nonbinary identity after happening upon the identity category in LGBTQIA+ digital spaces. The widespread availability of this information and this type of support is very new, which might explain the sense among some that nonbinary gender itself is something new. The accessibility of this information helped my interviewees to make sense of their gender. Moreover, several describe the discovery of the "nonbinary" gender label as a veritably salvific moment in their lives. At the time of this interview, Kazi was heavily involved in a leadership role in their university's Transgender Alliance group and committed to spreading awareness of transgender diversity. As a Muslim person of color, they report a strong investment in representing their intersectional identity for the sake of similarly marginalized groups.

Peyton, a 29-year-old white graduate student, experienced a similar gender journey from cis man to trans woman to nonbinary trans. Peyton is also very loud and proud about all of their identities, including their commitment to polyamory. Peyton never formally "came out" as queer to their parents; rather, they were outed by a well-meaning guidance counselor in high school who was allegedly worried about their mental health. Peyton's highly religious mother then kicked them out of the house and they went to live with their relatively more supportive father. Peyton recalls being bemused by the prevailing assumption at their high school that queer folk were pedophiles and the strict surveillance they found themselves under after the outing. Once Peyton was in a position to more fully explore their identity, they defaulted to living as a trans woman:

> I did do hormone replacement therapy and I have lived as a woman. And I did that in part because I felt pressured to do so. I felt like if I wanted to express my gender identity, it would be easier if everyone just assumed I was a woman. But, doing all of that—spending all that money and all of that pain and all of that effort in trying to appear one way—it didn't fulfill me anymore. It just gave me permission to be more of myself openly, according to social roles. And then I eventually said "Fuck that!" And I quit.

Peyton, like Kazi, is invested in spreading awareness of transgender diversity so other people know that they have other options beyond the binary. Both Peyton and Kazi blame transnormative messages for their decisions to undertake costly and painful steps toward binary transitioning. Through this process, they both realized that one binary gender felt as restrictive as the other. Ultimately, they both rejected their self-enforced accountability to the transgender binary, while maintaining their claim to membership within the transgender identity category—but specifically as "nonbinary transgender."

Not everyone in this ambivalent group formerly identified as a trans man or a trans woman; rather, the majority simply feel squeamish for one reason or another about claiming the transgender label. Some worry that they are not "trans enough," while others report concerns about appropriating another group's experience. Ashton, a 23-year-old white New Yorker is one such person. Ashton was very easy to talk to, with a striking appearance. They wore dark-rimmed glasses and their hair was short cropped and dark on the sides with a long blonde forelock. They had a nose ring, large gaged earrings on each lobe, and several other piercings along their ear rims. They wore a white T-shirt, a gold chain necklace, several bracelets, and a watch. Although Ashton feels confident in their nonbinary gender, they feel appropriative when they use the transgender label: "Sometimes I say that I'm nonbinary trans, but I usually just prefer to say I'm nonbinary because I'm not trying to be appropriative. I'm trying to watch where I walk." Ashton acknowledges the reality that most people associate the transgender label with the binary transitioning narrative, though they clarify that this does not apply to them.

It appears that the "umbrella" qualifier helps nonbinary people to "redo" transgender beyond the binary confines of trans man/trans woman; however, it simultaneously creates an illusion of unity that simply does not exist. Depending upon which transgender model people hold themselves accountable to, people position themselves differently under this imagined umbrella: some are completely covered in the center, while others prefer a position along the periphery. Even this latter peripheral contingent is split, between those who believe that they have not earned a position in the center and those who aren't sure whether they want to be under the umbrella at all. It would be inaccurate and even offensive to some, to automatically categorize them under the label transgender. What they are is nonbinary, a category that includes but is not limited to transgender people.

Gender Labels

In some ways, it is easier for my interviewees to explain what they aren't than what they are. This is because there is no consensus as to what any gender identity label means. Before I launched my interviews, I conducted preliminary research in a Reddit forum for Genderqueer people. People asked questions such as "How do I know if I'm femme presenting nonbinary or just regular ol bisexual cisgender?" and "Am I Genderqueer? Please Help!" The general consensus was that anyone who feels uncomfortable with binary identity categories is nonbinary by default; however, whether or not that makes them genderqueer is a matter of debate. This is because "genderqueer" is but one of the several popular nonbinary identity categories/labels; others that members invoke include agender, aliagender, androgynous, bigender, demigirl/demiguy, genderfluid, genderflux, genderfuck, gender variant, intergender, neutrois, polygender, and pangender. While some maintain that the different nuances matter, others understand these subcategories of nonbinary gender to be essentially interchangeable; therefore, they identify with multiple labels simultaneously.

Similarly, in my interviews people express ambivalence about the labels that they use for their gender. When I asked them to clarify their gender labels for me at the beginning of our conversation, most people mentioned more than one. Labels include: "nonbinary" ($n = 34$), "genderqueer" ($n = 27$), "genderfluid" ($n = 7$), "agender" ($n = 4$), "gender non-conforming" ($n = 3$), and "Two-Spirited" ($n = 3$). Genderqueer and nonbinary were by far the most commonly reported gender identity labels within my sample—a total of 39 respondents mentioned one or the other of these two labels if not both of them, among their list of identifiers. Most of these interviewees indicate that the two labels are virtually interchangeable, but some ($n = 13$) maintain that there are important differences between the two. These perceived differences are very real to those who identify explicitly as one or the other, though the differences that people report are oftentimes contradictory.

It is important to acknowledge that the label "genderqueer" can be *un*appealing to those who do not identify their sexuality as queer. Logan, a white 35-year old explains: "I also find that the term genderqueer really seems to me to conflate gender identity and sexual orientation. And I just find nonbinary to be a better term for me." Logan, who was assigned female at birth and is exclusively attracted to men, identifies their sexuality as "andro-sexual" as opposed to "queer" or "straight." For Logan, "nonbinary" draws an important distinction between their gender and their sexuality. Jes also reports discomfort with the inclusion of "queer" within "genderqueer," albeit for different reasons. A white 24-year-old Danish graduate student, Jes has never associated with the queer community:

> I actually identify more as nonbinary. And I think I do that because the word "queer" to me sounds…I associate it with …Maybe colors and glitter and people that are kinda sparkly and go to Gay Pride and are part of that envi-ronment, that I'm not really of it yet. Maybe I will be in the future, but I think nonbinary is more neutral? And I don't associate it with any kind of stereotype. I just associate it with the person who doesn't want to fit into a specific gender.

Jes, who is from a rural Scandinavian island, has largely experienced their gender and sexuality in isolation (and has evidently internalized some homo-phobic tropes along the way). Jes's quote demonstrates how the act of self-labeling is also an act of laying claim—or disavowing claim—to group membership within that label's corresponding community.

After genderqueer and nonbinary, the third most popular label among my interviewees is genderfluid ($n = 7$). Again, the difference between gender-fluid and genderqueer/nonbinary seems to mainly revolve around a matter of semantics; nevertheless, seven respondents including Hayden explicitly prefer the term genderfluid because they feel that it more accurately reflects their experience of their gender. Hayden arrived for their interview at my office in person, wearing jeans and a red flannel button-up shirt. They had brown middle-parted medium-length hair, dark-rimmed glasses, unplucked eyebrows, and no makeup. A white 21-year-old undergraduate student, Hayden had only been "out" about their gender for a year or two at the time of this interview. Nevertheless, they were eager to talk about their gender. Hayden eloquently explained why genderfluid is the best label for them:

> I do feel like my gender identity is very fluid. And yes, arguably, genderqueer is the same type of meaning. But the word fluid…it just sounded really well. And I really felt like that's where I fall. Like, I'm not in one or the other, or anywhere concretely in-between. I'm just shifting around constantly. And it made sense to me. And it doesn't feel like it's an unstable thing, but I'm stably fluid, if that makes sense. [...] There are definitely some days where I'm feeling real feminine, I'll put on a dress. And then there are some days where it's like, I don't even want to think of the fact that I am biologically a woman. Like, it just, it bothers me some days, severely. And then there are days where I don't feel like I'm anything on either side and I'm just kind of in-between. I don't even want to say it's days, because it's not like I wake up one morning and it's different, it can even be by the moment. Like, one moment I'll feel super feminine and the next I'll be like, "no."

Hayden's gender is constantly changing, from moment to moment. It is highly unpredictable and unstable and therefore difficult to label at all. However, if they have to pick a label and a corresponding community, "genderfluid" is the closest approximation. Kazi experiences their gender similarly: "I still am in a weird place with my gender. That's why I think genderfluid is pretty accurate. I fluctuate a lot between being nonbinary, being more masculine, being more feminine." Evidently, "genderfluid" is the only anticategorical label that enables Hayden and Kazi to feel liberated from the confines of a static gender identity. Through the use of "genderfluid," they can position themselves outside of the gender binary system without having to commit to any particular location.

Interviewees reported an affinity for other labels as well, that clarified the contours of their gender identity and experience. For example, Sydney, a white 32-year old, identifies as gender-neutral because, in their words, "I'm just kind of there on the gender spectrum." Carter, a reticent 20-year-old white undergraduate student, uses "agender" because "My situation is just feeling like I don't really have a connection to any gender at all, just like a person without any gender." Rhiannon, a conflict-averse white 24-year old, identifies as "grey-gender": "I guess I identify as grey-gender? Which is just kind of like a…just call it a shrug at gender generally." Not everyone feels so neutral about their gender or gender label, however. In lieu of a "shrug," Peyton prefers the "punch" of the label "genderfuck":

My preferred term that I use to talk to students, when I talk about trans issues and genderqueer issues, is the word genderfuck. I like the punch it has, and I like the fact that it has this sort of two-tone meaning: on the one half, it's kind of equivalent to genderqueer and on the other half, it kind of suggests that you're kind of screwed over by a system of gender. So genderfuck is perhaps the most fun.

Through such acts of self-labeling, people can quickly convey their political sentiments vis a vis the gender binary system.

Lastly, three people who I interviewed identify as "Two-Spirit," though only one of these three people is Native American: Justice. Justice has light brown skin, black wavy medium-length hair, short straight-across bangs, dark thick eyebrows, a septum piercing, and two silver hoops in the right nostril. They were born in the Czech Republic to a Latina mother and a Native American father, before moving to the state of Georgia in their teen years. Justice never felt uncomfortable about their gender until they arrived in the United States, at which point it became increasingly imperative that they claim a label. By the time of this interview, they had embraced identification as Two-Spirit, because it specifies their intersectionality as a nonbinary Native American person:

> I'm Two-Spirited. I'm part of the Two-Spirit society, which is the Native American queer community for people who do not identify within gender norms. Which I think is really important to me as a Native American woman, to be, to have a space as a Native American person rather than as a Native American woman. So that was really important. You know, gender binaries were transcribed onto native populations by colonizers. We originally did not have just woman and man genders. There were up to five identified genders in different tribes. And that transphobia, homophobia, queerphobia that exists in the Native American community, it comes from trying to fit within a mold from the colonizers. So, the Two-Spirit resurgence—we call it a resurgence because it's picked up speed recently—was really important to the native identity, but as well as queer identity, and the queer native identity.

Justice is actively engaged with their local Native American community and encouraged me to reach out to register with my tribes as well. Their excitement about reclaiming their heritage was frankly infectious and inspired me to consider it.

The act of alternative self-labeling is clearly an important component of "identity work" for nonbinary people. Self-labeling accomplishes numerous aims. This practice solidifies people's disidentification from the gender binary system, while specifying their particular gendered experience as well as their political investments. Some select labels that they understand to be politically neutral, while others, like Peyton, claim labels that they hope will communicate their antipathy toward the gender binary system. Although peoples' definitions of these labels oftentimes contradict one another, everyone provided some sort of answer when I asked which gender label they use—interestingly, this was not the case when I asked about pronouns.

Pronouns

As nonbinary people become increasingly vocal and visible in the general population, cisgender people increasingly encounter those who clarify upon introduction that they use the singular pronoun "they." However, cisgender people are often puzzled by the meaning of this pronoun, uncertain of its gendered implications or the reason why it even matters. This section aims to demystify the rationale behind nonbinary people's pronoun practices as well as the gendered identities that are associated with the singular "they" pronoun.

"They/them/theirs" is the most popular pronoun ($n = 39$) among my interviewees for a number of reasons. Some describe "they" as a logical preference. Jack, a white 26-year-old entrepreneur explains: "I like 'they' pronouns. It's not something I'm gonna have to explain to someone from scratch." Jack evidently thinks that, compared to pronouns like ze/zim/zer, they/them will be relatively familiar and easy for cisgender people to use. Addison, a white 26-year-old tech employee, also voices optimism about cisgender people's ability and willingness to adopt the singular use of "they":

> I use those because oftentimes when I'm introducing people to the idea of gender-neutral pronouns I can say, "Oh, well look, you use singular 'they' all the time when you don't know someone's gender." And then they go, "Oh, that's right" and it becomes easier for them to use that, rather than just simply referring to me as something which, for them, seems a little bit made up.

Jack and Addison hope that they might render themselves intelligible to cisgender people within the preexisting context by using pronouns that already have established meaning and cultural status.

A few people clarified that they are not enthusiastic about "they" pronouns, but use them anyway due to a lack of better gender-neutral pronoun options. Reagan, a white 32-year old who works for a queer Jewish organization explained:

I also don't necessarily identify with "they/them/their," but I feel like out of all of those options, of "he/him/hers," "she/her/hers," or "they/them/theirs," "they/them/theirs" fits me the most right now. Because "she/her/hers" really makes me uncomfortable, and so does "he/him/his." And "they/them/their" is less awkward for me.

Reagan had only begun to use these pronouns three weeks before our interview, although they had already had top surgery (breast tissue removal) and their family members already knew about their gender non-normativity. Drew, a white 23-year-old rabbinical student, uses "they" as a default as well, clarifying, "I would say there's no real connection to 'they' specifically, but more the idea of being unbounded and undefined." For both Drew and Reagan, "they" functions as a placeholder until more appropriate nonbinary pronouns come along.

Sam resolves their pronoun ambivalence by not voicing a preference at all. Sam is a friendly, well-spoken white Jewish 35-year old from the South. They have short-cropped sandy blonde hair, a big smile, and fair skin. Their story is particularly interesting for a number of reasons. Sam was kicked out of their house by their mother in high school when they "came out" as gay. They lived in various foster care homes while attending the same high school as their sister, who continued to live at home. When Sam turned 16, they filed for emancipation with the help of their father, who had been denied custody due to disability limitations. Sam persevered through this all, securing steady work as a healthcare professional and even eventually having a child on their own. When I asked them to clarify their pronouns at the beginning of our interview, they dismissively chuckled:

> I am just Sam and I don't have any preferred pronouns. I pretty much leave that up to whoever I'm talking to. Some people perceive me as more masculine, some people perceive me as more feminine. I sort of leave that to whatever they're comfortable with. I don't really feel like I need a particular, you know, designated pronoun.

Sam and others like Sam would prefer to be called by Sam's name instead of by a pronoun; however, Sam knows that people will inevitably insist on using pronouns since the overuse of names is very uncomfortable (as in this sentence). Sam leaves the pronoun choice up to the speaker, allegedly out of apathy.

And yet, in the gender binary system, this refusal to specify pronouns is inherently political. Peyton acknowledges that their refusal to specify pronouns is an act of self-conscious protest against forced binary gender categorization. Peyton is aware that such a refusal to specify pronouns makes people uncomfortable. Peyton hopes that this discomfort will force people to critically reflect upon their need to categorize strangers at all:

> As a personal policy, I do not enforce gender pronouns in any way, shape, or form. There's a couple of reasons for that…So the first reason, for me, is that I think if you are—if you are enforcing gender pronouns, and especially he or she, in some ways you're just reinforcing the same binary that you are trying to escape or leave, or otherwise resist. So, it doesn't make a whole lot of sense to me. I also think that when you…when someone asks the question, like, "What are your preferred gender pronouns?" My thought back is, "This is a question to make you comfortable with my experience of gender. It's not my gender's responsibly to make you comfortable. So, it doesn't have to fit into your rule set." So, by simply kind of tossing the question back to them and saying, "I'm not—I'm not going to provide you that easy answer," it doesn't let the other person off the hook, in terms of thinking about gender and what gender pronouns are actually doing to people.

Peyton does not identify with any of the available pronoun options, in part because these pronouns arose within the context of the gender binary system. Even pronouns like "they" or "ze" are problematic to Peyton because they are considered "alternative" in relation to a cisgender binary norm. Peyton feels significant social pressure to select one of these limited pronouns so that others can make sense of them within the context of the gender binary system. However, Peyton does not wish to make sense within that system; therefore, Peyton refuses to cooperate.

Five others are more flexible about pronouns than Peyton, so long as they aren't being referred to by the pronoun that corresponds with their birth sex/gender. Jesse is a white Jewish 26-year old living in San Francisco with their parents. They have light skin, dark eyebrows, medium-length dark brown hair, and a nice smile. A main theme throughout Jesse's interview was exasperation with being misgendered as a woman and their frustration with the very notion of a "queer look," especially in San Francisco. When I asked about their pronouns, they replied:

> Yeah, so I use "they/their" pronouns. I identity as nonbinary, and—I don't know if this is a result of being a nonbinary person or not being comfortable enough, or feeling like my gender is authentic enough. When someone uses feminine pronouns referring to me, I just kind of tighten up. And I feel like—gasp—am I not passing as a nonbinary person, you know?

Jesse interprets misgendering as a sign that they are failing at conveying their nonbinary gender to others. They are fine with being addressed by any other pronoun besides the one that corresponds with their birth sex/gender. In other words, they identify through what they are not—and they are not the sex/gender that was assigned to them at birth.

On the other side of the spectrum, nine people announced a preference—or at least a tolerance—for the binary pronouns that were assigned to them at birth. They simply consider it easier to use those pronouns and do not have faith in the public's willingness to understand nonbinary identities anyway, let alone respect the corresponding terminology. Jaylen is one such person, Jaylen is a white 25-year old who identifies as a genderqueer butch lesbian. They have light skin, buzzed dark blonde hair, and wore a black T-shirt during our interview. As Jaylen explains: "I've always had a hard time with pronouns. I don't use 'they/them' pronouns just 'cause…I don't know… I feel like it would be too much effort to get people to switch up. It would be a lot of anxiety on my part to try and train people. So, I go by 'she/her' pronouns." Jaylen would like to use a nonbinary pronoun, but holds back because they know that at the end of the day, they will be misgendered anyway. Jaylen suspects that even if they voiced an alternative preference, their request would be met with resistance.

Pronouns *can* be an integral piece of people's nonbinary gender identity, but this is not always the case. Some free themselves from the constraints of the gender binary system by opting out of pronouns altogether. Meanwhile, others decide they would rather save their energy for other battles and let people use whatever pronouns they wish. Simultaneously, a sizeable contingent of my interviewees identify very strongly with the gender-neutral singular "they" pronoun, at least as much as they identify with their gender label. The main takeaway is to never assume anything about anyone's pronouns without asking first, since even among nonbinary people, practices and preferences vary widely.

Conclusion

The journey of self-discovery for nonbinary people is long and oftentimes convoluted. People are raised with the message that everyone is either a boy or a girl, a man or a woman, and sometimes, exceptionally, a man or a woman who was born in the wrong body. The possibility of having a gender that evades this man/woman binary framework simply is not well-known, popularly embraced, or represented in the media culture. Because of this, nonbinary people have to try on other identities before realizing, often through a lengthy process of trial and error, that they are nonbinary. This chapter has illustrated this process of "identity work," that I call "rethinking sex and gender."

Why does this matter? The purpose of this book is to examine the microscale processes that are driving the social change that we see happening in the gender landscape surrounding us. This change does not happen without considerable labor from nonbinary people themselves, as they render themselves increasingly visible and contingently prompt others to reconceptualize the gender order. However, before they ever get to that point, they have to realize that they *are* nonbinary. As this chapter has demonstrated, this realization is no small task.

Although this internalized process is an impressive feat unto itself, it is only the beginning of the journey for nonbinary people. Without communicating their nonbinary gender to others, they will continue to experience misgendering as men and women multiple times per day every day of their lives. The next chapter focuses on this interpersonal level of accountability in nonbinary people's gender journeys. How do they convey a gender to others that others do not even know exists, or sometimes actively resist? How do they achieve recognition as nonbinary from people in their lives? These interpersonal interactions are key to the redoing gender process, as they prompt cisgender people to rethink and redo gender in their own daily lives. As later chapters will demonstrate, these interpersonal interactions seem to have created a ripple effect that is broadening gender consciousness.

Notes

1. For more, see Georgiann Davis's (2015) *Contesting Intersex.*
2. Snow and Anderson (1987).
3. The prevalence of non-heterosexual orientations among nonbinary people has been noted elsewhere. See Factor and Rothblum (2008), Kuper et al. (2012), and Callis (2014).
4. For the origins of the sexual-inversion stigma, see Krafft-Ebing's (1901) *Psychopathia Sexualis* and Havelock Ellis's (1911) *Studies in the Psychology of Sex.*
5. Schilt and Westbrook (2009).
6. For an in-depth exploration of "not trans enough" anxieties, see Garrison (2018) or Catalano (2015).
7. For more on the "transgender umbrella" strengths and limitations, see Davidson (2007); for more on conflicting definitions of transgender legitimacy, see Namaste (2000) or Roen (2002).
8. Johnson (2016) and Schilt and Lagos (2017).

Resignifying Gender

Many of the social interactions that nonbinary people experience in a given day happen during casual interactions with strangers. More often than not, these strangers attempt to categorize the nonbinary person as "man" or "woman" at first sight, a gender attribution process that determines the language they use to address the person throughout the rest of the interaction. People who comfortably identify as men or women may not realize how often we assume these gender identities of others through routine terminology (such as ma'am/sir, Miss/Mister, mother/father, sister/brother, girlfriend/boyfriend, wife/husband). However, nonbinary people notice very much. That is not to say that all nonbinary people are actively upset by the gendered assumptions within our language, but some do experience the daily barrage of casual misgendering as deeply distressing.

Nonbinary people oftentimes experience misgendering from strangers in the name of "manners." Problematically, so-called manners reflect the dominant group's values and norms. In this case, the dominant gender ideology posits that everyone is either a man or a woman and should be addressed as "sir" or "ma'am," respectively. Corey elaborates upon the harm that these seemingly neutral "manners" cause: "You're fighting against this culture of 'We need to be polite and need to be welcoming,' except that being polite and being welcoming looks different for other people." Corey has tried to correct those strangers with whom they have regular contact, but it has been to no avail—they continue to misgender Corey, while insisting that this microaggression is a straight-forward matter of "being polite." This institutionalization of misgendering through "manners" makes it extremely difficult for nonbinary people to confront strangers about using these labels.

Apparently, the act of identifying as nonbinary is not enough to avoid getting misgendered as a man or a woman. In order to achieve social recognition, one must also somehow convey this nonbinary gender to others. This chapter focuses on how nonbinary people navigate first impressions, through both visual and verbal means, to effectively communicate that they shouldn't be placed in the "man" or the "woman" box. Since first impressions are often visual, people in my sample invest considerable thought and time into cultivating gendered cues that mark themselves as neither/nor at first glance. Some have also changed their names to be more gender-neutral and/or specify nonnormative pronouns when introducing themselves to others. Through all of these practices, nonbinary people find ways to signify that their gender is not what strangers might assume.

I begin this chapter by detailing the labor that nonbinary people invest into verbally announcing themselves as nonbinary, with a focus on pronoun declaration. I hope that this section will convey to cisgender readers how scary and difficult it is for nonbinary people to do this in the first place, and the pain that it causes them when cisgender people refuse to honor these disclosures. This section should also make it clear that nonbinary people do not disclose their gender as often as they would like to, either due to safety concerns or due to sheer exhaustion.

Following this section on verbal cues, I switch my focus on visual cues that help people signal their gender non-normativity. Wardrobe and fashion alterations help people deviate from traditional masculine and feminine appearances. Many also style their hair in gender non-normative ways and change their body hair practices to challenge gender norms. Those assigned female at birth (AFAB) oftentimes grow their body hair and facial hair out, while those assigned male at birth (AMAB) oftentimes remove their facial and body hair, sometimes through the permanent hair removal process called "electrolysis." A few of my AFAB interviewees have also had "top surgery," while many more bind their chests flat and hope to pursue top surgery in the future. And finally, several people in this sample have begun hormone therapy regimens that help them feel and look less like the gender they were assigned at birth. Through all of these "body work"[1] practices, nonbinary people resignify their gender beyond the binary categories of "man" and "woman." This chapter will illuminate the thoughts and hopes behind these practices as well as nonbinary people's experiences of them.

Before delving into this chapter, I must emphasize that these resignification practices are not unique to nonbinary people; trans men and trans women go through similar processes during and after their gender transitions. Even some cisgender people who find themselves commonly misgendered must engage in pronoun specification and strategic wardrobe selection/grooming practices. What makes the nonbinary gender case study unique is that the end-goal for many people is to thwart categorization as "man" or as "woman" altogether. Given the commonplace assumption that everyone can be sorted into one of these two categories upon a glance, the nonbinary gender signification process requires serious thought, strategy, and insight into binary gender symbolism.

Pronoun Specification

After rethinking sex and gender and settling on a nonbinary gender for themselves, those who decide to use "they/them/their" pronouns find themselves facing the never-ending task of disclosing this pronoun to others, explaining what it means, and reminding people to use it when they inevitably slip up and misgender the nonbinary person after the fact. This process of "coming out" is ongoing, as is also the case for other members of the LGBTQIA+ community. However, due to the binary-gendered structure of the English language (and most languages), nonbinary people experience misgendering prompts to "come out" multiple times per day every single day. Some of my interviewees who use they/them/their pronouns don't bother to disclose this to other people, out of fear of rejection or due to fatigue; others selectively disclose to people whom they trust; and others assert their proper pronoun whenever they experience misgendering, as a matter of principle.

The decision to enforce gender-neutral pronoun use is one that people do not take lightly. Kai, a 25-year-old white graduate student, was still trying to muster the courage to tell their live-in partner about their gender at the time of this interview. They had experimented with using they/them/their pronouns occasionally, but always alongside she/her/hers pronouns, and always under the guise of apathy. Kai experiences misgendering as a woman most of the time, with increasing frustration:

> For a long time, I was saying that my preferred pronouns were "they/their" or "she/her" and then for a while I was saying I prefer "they/their," but I wasn't like offended by "she/her." And now I'm feeling like, "Ok I was just saying that to please the other people. And just like, be firm about what my actual pronoun preference is."

After using both pronouns for some time, Kai became increasingly uncomfortable. However, they were also uncomfortable with the fact that they would have to be extremely assertive to make their pronouns known: "I prefer that people use 'they/their,' but I don't think anyone knows that and I don't feel like there's space to talk about that."

Reagan, a white 32-year old from New York, went through a similar thought process regarding pronoun assertion: "The first part in [my email] signature was 'she/her/hers' and then I added 'they/them/their' and then I was kind of playing around with the order of preference. And then I was just like…I just was like, just do it." Reagan already had top surgery, but still felt timid about correcting people who misgendered them as a woman. Like Kai, Reagan dreads having to confront people about the fact that they are using the wrong pronouns for them. However, at a certain point, Kai and Reagan's fatigue of misgendering outweighs their conflict aversion.

People's gender disclosure strategies vary somewhat depending upon their political sentiments toward the gender binary system. While people like Kai and Reagan dread pronoun disclosure, others have accepted this act as a political duty in solidarity with other nonbinary people. Carson explains:

> Usually, I would say nine times out of ten when I'm misgendered, I do correct people. I think my partner sometimes will wish that I will let people misgender me a little more sometimes, just so that we can get treated better, more opportunities. But I do feel like I'm always calling people out. Like, trying to have a constructive conversation, trying to open up the idea, not because I want to rip everyone's head off. It's just because it's the reality and I think we need to talk about it.

Carson renders themselves vulnerable to harassment, violence, and malicious misgendering by being so vocal about their nonbinary pronouns. They acknowledge that their assertiveness about this matter sometimes borders on aggression. However, the personal is political for Carson; therefore, the energy is a worthwhile investment by their calculation. Jesse agrees that this labor is an important investment on political grounds: "I use 'they' and 'their' pronouns because they disrupt language. And especially in non-queer, non-trans spaces. It's a way of disrupting the normativity of those spaces and asserting my presence a little bit more. Even though there's labor involved in that."

Regardless of how often they correct people, my interviewees continue to experience frequent misgendering in their daily lives, even from their friends, family, and acquaintances. Hunter, a nineteen-year-old mixed-race college student, voiced their exasperation with this scenario while talking with me in my office:

> I've had a lot of people asking stupid questions or refusing to listen to me when I say I use "they" pronouns. Like, I introduce myself that way every single time. There is, like, a group introduction or an introduction to someone I haven't met before. Like, every time. The reminding after that is hard for me.

Hunter was relatively new to the nonbinary "coming out" experience at the time of this interview, having only realized they were nonbinary three months prior. They wore dark-rimmed glasses, a beanie with fake black curled bangs, a sleeveless flannel button-down shirt, and a nose piercing. Hunter wants to correct instances of misgendering among their friends and acquaintances when they occur, but this corrective labor has already become unbearably painful.

Dakota has had a similar experience, but recently became more assertive about their pronouns anyway. A white 31-year-old high school teacher in the Bay Area, Dakota has shoulder-length middle-parted brown wavy hair and unplucked eyebrows. They were wearing a colorful blouse with dangly earrings during our interview. As they explained:

> I started being more proactive about pronouns in the last two or three years, mostly since my child was born. I felt really like—all of a sudden, in a way that I hadn't quite felt before—I felt really a kind of disjunction, of like an unpleasantness around the word father and that parenting role. And I realized that I needed to articulate this in a wider way, for people to understand that this is part of who I am. Since then, if someone in my life that I'm close to, that kind of has that kind of Trans Level 101 education, then I feel like "Great! These are my pronouns..." and for everybody else, I would kind of internally roll my eyes, but not really make any deal out of it. Since then, I've started kind of putting my foot down a little bit more, saying to the people in my life at this time, "You've had this, this isn't new, I've been asking you this for years, you can do it, I believe in you."

Dakota used to compartmentalize, holding different types of people accountable to different standards. However, after a certain period of time, they feel like people should interact with them appropriately, especially given the considerable amount of coaching labor that Dakota has invested into achieving recognition.

Cameron also feels like people's reluctance or refusal to use their pronouns is not a matter of difficulty so much as antipathy. Cameron is a white 20-year old from Denmark with a striking appearance. They have shoulder-length brown hair with bangs, a unibrow and beard, and a septum piercing as well as a tongue piercing. They routinely try to get cisgender people to respect their they/them/their pronouns, but to little avail: "I get a lot of people that challenge me on the grammar end of it. They'll be like 'Well, that's not grammatically correct,' which it actually it is. But I feel like that's not what it's really about anyway. They're just trying to derail the conversation I think." According to Cameron, the effort that it takes for a cisgender person to remember and use a gender-neutral pronoun is nothing compared to the effort it takes a nonbinary person to withstand near-constant invalidation in their daily lives. And yet, when nonbinary people speak up and try to get their needs met, cisgender people react defensively, complaining that it is "too hard." As though cisgender people are the victims when they are misgendering nonbinary people.

The decision to clarify pronouns and thereby announce oneself to strangers is deeply personal—there is no right or wrong course of action. This decision requires significant thought and trepidation either way, and it constitutes a form of labor that goes unseen by cisgender people. Given how vocal cisgender critics of nonbinary pronouns have been, it is important to shed light on the other side of the interaction—the fear of rejection that nonbinary people must overcome to even arrive at the point of announcing their pronouns in the first place.

Aesthetics

Most people in my sample changed the way that they dressed when they realized they were nonbinary. Fashion is a relatively easy and accessible way to change the gendered messages that someone sends about themselves to others. As K shares, "I realized what I wanted was for people to not know, or to have to ask, or like stumble a bit before they said something." If someone wants to challenge strangers' default gendering of them as "man" or "woman," they can err toward an androgynous "look" or mix and match visual cues that are associated with masculinity and femininity. Or they can go out of their way to cultivate an aesthetic that is unambiguously masculine or feminine, in order to avoid getting misgendered as the sex/gender assigned to them at birth.

Although many nonbinary people describe their fashion as androgynous, their interpretation of androgyny differs. Several AFAB people described androgyny as interchangeable with masculinity, while no AMAB people described it this way. When Sequoia studied abroad in Armenia, for example, they felt freer to experiment with their identity and corresponding appearance. Away from their mother for the first time, they finally sought out an LGBTQ community that encouraged self-expression:

> Being in Armenia made me dress very feminine, which made me feel very bad. But those are the standards for a woman in such a Catholic conservative world. But then I could also feel really—when I was within the LGBT community, to start wearing bowties or ties or to start wearing man's shirts, or to look for a more androgynous look that would actually make me look in the mirror and say like, "Wow, I feel—I never thought I would feel this comfortable in my life, or so beautiful or so sexy or just so good with myself."

Sequoia understands their change in self-expression to be a shift toward androgyny, even though they describe it as the appropriation of masculine-associated accessories—like bowties, ties, and men's shirts. This conflation was common among AFAB interviewees and possibly even within the broader AFAB nonbinary community, as Addison suggests: "In the past year I've been sort of thinking about why, in order to present as androgynous, the trend has been more towards—especially among white people—the trend has been towards really emphasizing masculinity. It's like, masculine can go either way, but feminine can only be read as feminine."[2] However, anecdotally it seems that this pendulum swing levels out after a time, as people become more comfortable with their gender and begin to reintroduce select feminine elements into their wardrobes. For example, Kazi, who used to identify as a trans man, explains:

> I took a long time, like a little break. Time to really explore femininity again, to see, like, is it really... Is it me who doesn't identify with it, or is it just like me having this... All this specific media ideals of what it is to be man and what it is to be androgynous. Like, androgyny is always masculinity in a slightly different form. Really rarely you see... Even the most, like... Even androgynous men, the ones who are slightly feminized, they still have a very strong sense of masculinity to them. So, I always was a little confused about it, and I needed to take the time to know if I could still identify with what I identify and still present femininely.

When AFAB people like Kazi realize that they are not women, it might be difficult for them to continue wearing clothes or accessories that they associate with that identity. And yet, dressing and looking "masculine" also feels wrong to many AFAB nonbinary people. As we saw in the previous chapter, it tends to be much easier for people to identify what they are *not* than what they *are*. This disidentification process, which is so crucial to helping people navigate the flowchart of identities, also manifests through fashion choices.

The masculine/androgynous clothes that AFAB people tend to wear do not similarly help AMAB people convey their gender non-conformity to strangers. Instead, they must adopt feminine elements into their wardrobe in order to accomplish this same aim. The challenge that my AMAB interviewees report is the desire to avoid looking like a drag queen. This is not to say that my interviewees look down upon drag; indeed, several experimented with drag before realizing that they were nonbinary and credit their involvement with the drag community for their realization.[3] The concern is rather that drag is a form of entertainment and not necessarily meant to reflect the person's actual identity. When Mason, for example, realized that dressing up was not just for fun, but an actual form of self-expression, they felt a sudden need to "tone it down":

> I started wearing nail polish on the weekends and then slowly started incorporating some more subtle makeup…still wearing a little bit of BB creams or not quite full-coverage foundation, like lighter coverage. Doing a little bit of eyeshadow and a little bit of eyeliner. And then I've been sort of working my way up from there. And wearing women's shoes out and that kind of thing. So, I'm still sort of building up the courage to go outside in skirts and dresses and that kind of thing. Which is kind of funny because when I did drag, I mean it was very nerve-wracking to go out in drag. But now that I'm stepping back from drag, it's kind of…sort of stepping back from that whole over-the-top femininity and I'm trying to move more towards the more androgynous presentation. Suddenly the idea of wearing women's clothes is a lot more intimidating.

Although Mason is by no means new to expressing their femininity, things have changed since they realized that they are nonbinary. They do not want people to think they are being silly and they certainly do not want to feel like they are making fun of themselves. Their transition from drag queen to nonbinary transfemme requires careful consideration and experimentation with feminine signifiers.

In some ways, revamped wardrobes constitute an equal opportunity for people to announce their nonbinary gender. However, as this section has illustrated, fashion is still limited in its power to effectively thwart the binary gender system and convey a nonbinary gender identity. Perhaps as a result of clothing's limited semiotic power, the nonbinary people in my sample also reported self-conscious changes to their hair as a key component to their nonbinary gender expression.

Head Hair

The fact that so many people change their hair after realizing that they are nonbinary should not come as a surprise. Hair is remarkably binary-gendered.[4] Stereotypically, men have short hair and women have long hair; men have hairy bodies and women are supposed to have hairless bodies; older men have gray hair, but women do not.[5] Furthermore, there are strong cultural associations between women's long hair and their femininity.[6]

As a result of this binary symbolism, the moment when AFAB people cut off their long hair proves to be a transformational rite of passage. Respondents associate long hair with the prescribed femininity that they have long since rejected: "I don't have specific reasons why I cut my hair shorter, it just felt like the right thing to do. That I was letting go of someone who I was trying to be that I couldn't be" (Harley, white, 30). Similarly, Sydney (white, 32) describes their first short haircut as "a symbol, or the first thing, that suggested that maybe this box that people have been trying to put me in is not the right one for me."

Long hair proved to be exceptionally burdensome for Hunter (Black/ White/ Native American, 19): as a mixed-race individual with African heritage, part of their socially mandated feminine ritual included straightening their otherwise curly hair in emulation of the white beauty standard.[7] They describe the moment when they finally cut their hair as a concrete moment of gender actualization:

> My friend took the clippers by the hand and was like "Alright, sit down." That was more, "You know who you are. You know what to do to make you feel good and I want to help you get to that place." And I remember I was watching my hair fall into this bag that we were holding in front of my face—'cause I was sitting at a table with my head down like this—and we had a bag in front of me and the machine going forward into it. And I was watching all of my hair fall into that bag and I just started to feel really great.

With the support of their friend, Hunter cut away the yoke of femininity that had kept them from embodying their authentic self: as their friend so insightfully said, "You know who you are." Hunter describes their long hair as a visible signifier that prevented them from communicating their gender to the world and from feeling their gender within themselves. They later elaborated:

> When I had longer hair, I just felt attached to that hair and I was like...I remember I was stroking my hair, and I was like, "This is what's stopping

people from understanding that I'm not just female. Like, this is what's stopping them." [...] Shaving my head was the moment that I became comfortable enough with myself to not try to deny it and say "Oh no, I'm just a really masculine girl."

As long as they kept their hair long, Hunter felt as though they were signaling permission to others to treat them as a woman. By changing their physical body, Hunter was able to alter this signal and breathe new life into their nonbinary social body.

For some people, like Harley, this type of signal change worked as a way to avoid getting misgendered as a woman:

I have been identified as male and referred to as "they" since I cut my hair short a couple of years ago. When I'm traveling, sometimes people identify me as male. And I think people aren't always sure of my pronouns, so sometimes they just use "they" to kind of catch all. And I find that people ask me more than they used to. So, there's an interesting intersection, where if people look genderqueer or they look different from what you might expect their pronoun to be, people are more likely to ask.

Harley's short hair signifies that there is something queer about them—though whether that queerness is gendered or sexual remains unclear to some. As Harley further explained: "I think that since I cut my hair, more women notice me. So, as far as sexuality goes, I think I'm definitely assumed to be queer more often." This quote illustrates the "blurry intersection"[8] between sex, gender, and sexuality, as Harley's gender non-conforming hair cut also evidently signifies lesbian group identification. Indeed, Jordan (white, 24) avoids cutting their hair short precisely so they will not be misrecognized as a lesbian: "When I have really short hair people will see me as a lesbian because a lot of lesbians in Denmark have short hair [...] I don't want to identify with that environment." Jordan goes on to explain that the lesbian community in Denmark is rife with transphobic feminists and they wish to achieve as much distance as possible from that community.

Justice's high school peers also mistakenly assumed that they were a lesbian, simply due to the way that they mixed gendered aesthetics in their wardrobe. These peers did not understand the distinction between gender and sexuality that allows for feminine lesbians, masculine heterosexual women, and nonbinary AFAB people who prefer AMAB partners. As a result of this constant social misrecognition at a young age, Justice misidentified as a lesbian for quite some time: "A lot of my gender identity in high school was—my gender and my sexuality identity—was transcribed onto me, rather than chosen by me." Justice's experience demonstrates how gender and sexuality become entangled within binary gender ideology. It did not occur to people (including Justice) that Justice might be nonbinary, because they were not even aware that nonbinary gender existed. However, they *were* familiar with the concept of a lesbian, and that is how they made sense of Justice's deviance from binary gender ideals.

To avoid getting misrecognized as a lesbian, most AFAB people in my sample embrace hair styles that they consider neither feminine nor masculine. For example, Hunter styled their hair in a Mohawk for a while: When I got the Mohawk I was like, boys and girls have Mohawks. Boys and girls have long Mohawks too. That, for me, was the first step in like saying "Ok, I don't have to worry about this not being feminine or not being masculine." Harley also tries to accomplish a gender-bending "look," by combining short hair with long hair: "I like the asymmetry thing. It kind of lets me be both at the same time of like having a somewhat feminine look and also have a more butch look."

Indeed, several of my interviewees shave part of their hair while keeping other sections longer; this asymmetrical aesthetic has become so ubiquitous among nonbinary people that Justice (Native American/ Latinx, 26) considers it to be a reliable way to identify like-minded others: "I think partially shaved heads definitely signify certain parts of identity. Like if you see somebody on the subway with a partially shaved head and part is long, you can almost positively assume there's something alternative in their lifestyle." Justice goes on to explain why asymmetry is such a powerful signifier of queer group membership:

I have a rat tail that's significantly longer than the rest of my hair and I keep it because I think of it as a signifier. Anything to distance myself from straight heteronormative ideologies of beauty, without compromising my own aesthetic, I think is really important. So, if you have a fully asymmetric hairline, like, whether it's short here and then long here, in the States it's a big signifier, whether being queer or alternative or being outside of the norm.

Any sort of visual rejection of the feminine beauty ideal is a useful signifier of queer identity, according to Justice.

Reciprocally, long hair usefully functions as a way for AMAB people to "hint" at their gender within spaces that otherwise pressure gender conformity, such as the workplace. For example, Avery (white, 28) shares: "I started thinking about that, if I can't professionally dress up, I don't feel comfortable dressing up in a professional environment like the University, then I may as well use my hair as a way of expressing myself." Although Avery feels pressure to wear clothing that conforms to masculine codes of professionalization, they feel safe enough to rebel through their asymmetrical hair style.

The solution for some genderfluid AMAB people in my sample is to cut their hair short but wear wigs on "feminine" days: "For me, when I want to present androgynously so people read me as such, I would go for perhaps a sweater of some sort. But generally, if I go for feminine clothing, I would go for a full dress or skirt, makeup, a wig, rings, stuff like that" (Cameron, white, 20). Lisa (white, 61) also wears wigs while maintaining a playful relationship with gender:

> A lot of the times I wear makeup and wigs and everything like that, so that's something I've been doing since I joined the Radical Fairies. I love wigs and I love my own hair because it's silver and I like to—this past Easter, I have an Easter service where I had my normal hair and full make up and everything. But tomorrow I'm going to be doing a church service at a church community in Manhattan and I'm going to be wearing a wig and a suit and everything, a women's suit and all of that.

As a self-employed performer, Lisa is not overly concerned about "passing" as a cisgender woman or presenting their gender in a cohesive manner. However, Lisa's occupational circumstances are exceptional within this sample.

Body and Facial Hair

The vast majority of my AFAB respondents reported that they stopped engaging in body hair removal—a quintessentially feminizing body practice[9]—when they stopped identifying as women. Some hope to signify their non-normative gender through this act of resistance: "I do like when people see my underarm hair because I'm hoping they'll be like—I don't care if they're offended or anything, but it does send a signal of sorts that, you know, I don't care or that I'm—because it is, unfortunately, it's like a radical statement. Just to have underarm hair" (Ashton). Ashton (white, 23) understands their body hair to "send a signal of sorts" about their gender. However, whether this signal is received as conveying gender non-normativity or feminist politics remains beyond their control.[10]

Of course, body hair gender norms do not only affect women and nonbinary AFAB people. Masculinity and maleness are also generally associated with hairiness. Therefore, the removal of body hair can help some AMAB people distance themselves from feeling masculine and signifying masculinity, as Dakota (white, 31) explains: "I shave legs and arms, and so anytime that those appendages are visible then that's kind of a signifier, even if it's a subtle one." Significantly, AMAB people's ability to signify gender non-normativity through hairlessness is easier for some than others. Parker (Filipinx, 29), who is Asian American, does not grow very much body hair or facial hair. They note that their natural hairlessness enables them to signify a more androgynous appearance: "I mean I've always had very little body hair so that kind of helps you know."

The binary-gendered symbolism associated with facial hair further problematizes AMAB people's ability to avoid misgendering; therefore, it is not particularly surprising that most AMAB people in this sample remove this gendered matter. However, it should be noted that struggles with facial hair vary by race. Parker plucks rather than shaves the few hairs that they grow on their face. Meanwhile, plucking is not even an option for Cameron, who grows a considerable amount of hair on their face: "I don't like associating with anything that could be masculine which is why my ever-constant growing beard is annoying the hell out of me." By cultivating extreme hairlessness, AMAB people can embody at least one visual component of "emphasized femininity"[11]; however, permanent hairlessness is an expensive and time-consuming pursuit that few AMAB individuals can afford. As a result of the cost associated with electrolysis, most AMAB individuals endure their struggle with the masculine semiotics of facial hair stubble on an ongoing basis.

Due to these same binary-gendered stereotypes, several AFAB interviewees voiced an appreciation for facial hair growth. By growing facial hair, AFAB people are able to alter their physical body into better alignment with their nonbinary-gendered social bodies. As Piper (Arabic, 22) shares, "One of the goals during my transition is also I'd like some kind of beard at least even for a little bit." It should be noted, though, that some female interviewees have always grown facial hair, hence the fallacy of the binary-gendered stereotype in the first place. For example, Corey (white, 28) has always grown perceptible facial hair:

I was always a hairy person. I've always had this little beard, as it were. I know some other people with PCOS [poly-cystic ovarian syndrome] who have much more severe, sort of facial hair issues, of which those people aren't—like, some of them are not at all gender non-conforming. They are totally happy being cis people but it's just something that they have to deal with. And so, it's like, "Oh great, more hair. Woo. What's the difference? I've always been hairy."

The prospect of growing more facial hair once they began their testosterone regiment was underwhelming for Corey. And yet, other AFAB people in my sample who did not have similar pre-transition experiences with facial hair found the prospect of growing a beard or a mustache to be very exciting and gender-affirming.

The term "facial hair" does not always include eyebrows, but in this case, eyebrows also feature as a gender signifier that people manipulate to send particular gender cues. Thin eyebrows are generally indicative of femininity within United States culture, while thicker eyebrows are generally indicative of masculinity (though thick eyebrows periodically become fashionable for women). When Jordan wishes to incorporate more masculine elements into their feminine-of-center appearance, they use cosmetics to make their eyebrows appear fuller. Reciprocally, Dakota (AMAB) explains: "I'll get my eyebrows waxed and I've liked that in terms of communicating androgyny." Eyebrow grooming is such a gendered practice that these slight modifications can help nonbinary people confuse or problematize binary gender attribution.

Binding/Top Surgery

Even if AFAB people cut their hair short, grow out their body hair, and stop plucking their eyebrows, they still struggle to avoid misgendering if they have visibly full chests. This secondary sex characteristic presents a gender-attribution obstacle that can be difficult for people to overcome, as this section will demonstrate. Not all AFAB people are bothered by their chests, but it features as a commonly encountered barrier to social recognition among my interviewees. Some "bind" their chests to overcome this obstacle, while others experience so much distress in relation to their full chests that they decide to surgically remove the breast tissue altogether. Because this section focuses on visual cues that help people avoid misgendering, I will focus on the aesthetic benefits of binding and "top surgery" here; however, that is not to say that all AFAB people engage in these practices or that everyone who engages in them experiences the distressing sensation called "body dysphoria."

Crucially, some people who would like to bind cannot, as Sydney explained to me. Sydney is a heavy-set white 32-year old with a large chest. They like to play with gendered cues, but are limited in their ability to signify masculinity due to their chest's prominence:

> They're quite literally too big to bind. You know, I try binding them and they're still these huge lumps of stuff on top. Like it's never gonna look flat

or even vaguely flat. I mean, they're gonna look like breasts squished to my chest which just looks weird and it's uncomfortable. And I would rather, just you know, wear a bra and have them supported properly and wear jeans and t-shirts most of the time.

Sydney has had to give up on binding because it is a logistical impossibility. They haven't totally ruled out top surgery, but they explained to me that they are "surgery-phobic" and would have to get over their fear before seriously considering it.

Addison, a white 26-year old, finds binding to be prohibitively uncomfortable. Instead, they wear sports bras that are a couple of sizes too small, which compress their chest and make it appear flatter. Unlike Sydney, Addison has not ruled out top surgery:

> I feel 90% confident about moving forward with a thing like top surgery. Again, because I want to get out of passing privilege. I really want to confuse things. If I do that, then my relationship with my fashion is gonna change. I will feel much more comfortable wearing skirts and things like that because, again, the goal is just to confuse the fuck out of people.

As it stands, Addison relies on masculine-encoded fashion to signify their nonbinary gender to people. They feel certain that strangers would gender them as a woman due to their chest if they did not wear such clothing. They suspect that without their chest, they would feel freer to reincorporate feminine-encoded fashion back into their wardrobe and play with gender a bit more.

Meanwhile, some AFAB people struggle to wear the "men's clothes" that they would like to wear to express themselves because the clothes do not fit properly on their chests. When Reagan initially realized that they were nonbinary, they invested in a whole new wardrobe of "men's clothes" before discovering this issue of fit: "I bought all of these clothes because they were the style that I wanted to have, but I never wore them because I was never confident in my body so it was just like…it felt pointless to wear clothes if I didn't like the way they looked on me." Reagan's body dysmorphia led them to try to lose as much weight as possible so their curves would disappear, but their discontent remained. They ultimately recovered from this eating disorder and opted for top surgery. Later that year, they got a new job and went shopping for a new wardrobe once more. This time was different:

> My girlfriend was helping me pick out a bunch of clothes or outfits for my first week at work and I started crying 'cause I was like, "Holy shit! This is how

I've always wanted to look!" And it was another one of those moments of, like, I feel like home, I finally see myself in my reflection. Like, I actually look in the mirror now and before I would avoid the mirror 'cause I hated seeing my chest. And now I will stand in the mirror and I don't cross my arms anymore and I kind of stand like…you can't see it, but I kind of stand with my chest out a little bit just 'cause I'm so proud of how I look now.

Reagan never felt like themselves or looked the way they wanted with their unwanted breast tissue. They couldn't even look in the mirror because all they could see was a woman looking back. Without a full chest, Reagan is finally able to dress in more male-tailored clothes and achieve the transmasculine aesthetic that they've always wanted. In order to feel and look nonbinary, Reagan and others in this study needed to remove this unwanted feminized bodily matter.

Hormones

Besides top surgery, hormone replacement therapy (HRT) can help nonbinary people modify the gendering of their bodies. HRT regimens prescribe testosterone to those who were assigned female at birth and estrogen (along with testosterone blockers) to those who were assigned male at birth. After a period of time, these hormones begin to change people's bodies in subtle and not so subtle ways that have the effect of helping the person feel and look less like the gender that was assigned to them at birth. Not everyone who gets top surgery also goes on hormone replacement therapy and not everyone who undergoes HRT also gets top surgery. It is particular to the individual, their experience of their gender, their desired gendered appearance, and their experience (or lack thereof) of body dysmorphia. Some people pursue this hormone regimen primarily due to a desire to feel more like their gender, while others are motivated by the appearance factor. Jordan is in the latter camp: "I hate when people call me 'she' and 'her.' And they do, right, because I look like a woman. So, maybe later on I would like to try testosterone to see what that does to my body and the way I pass in public."

Hormones affect people in different ways, as Corey experienced and observed firsthand. As someone with polycystic-ovarian syndrome, Corey had always had more facial hair than other females. They suspect that their propensity toward hairiness has helped testosterone have a rapidly visible affect on their body:

I went to a gender liberated pool party and I was looking around and I noticed that I kept staring at all of the transmasculine people's chest hair and lack of chest hair. Because I looked down and I had seen some chest hair and I was like, "Holy shit!" I've been on T for two and a half months and I already have some chest hair even though the quality of mine isn't like a lot of other people's. It's just sort of dark skin hair that's there. But I'm looking around at people who have been on T forever and they don't have chest hair and I guess they didn't get the hairy genes like I did, so it was interesting.

Only two months in, Corey already had significantly more chest hair than other people on testosterone. However, other changes that are typically associated with testosterone use were slower to develop for Corey, such as a lower vocal register. They surmise that they simply have the "hair gene" that some other people lack.

For most people, physical changes on hormones are much more gradual. Lane has been on hormones for eight months and feels like the change in their appearance has happened so slowly that it's been difficult to appraise: "I don't know, like, I have no idea how people gender me. It feels like I'm in this gradual stage of people… well, people are now starting to not gender me as female which is very interesting. But yeah, I guess I look pretty regular. I haven't experienced any mega big stuff." Clearly, everyone experiences hormones differently. However, they do tend to help people feel and look less like the gender that was assigned to them at birth. This is a step that people do not take lightly. Once the bodily changes begin, people begin to feel and look more nonbinary and experience less misgendering than they contended with beforehand.

Contingencies

My AMAB interviewees expressed significantly more fear and trepidation about visually expressing themselves than AFAB people did. This difference makes sense since trans women are more vulnerable toward violent hate crimes than trans men.[12] Men and those who are assigned male at birth experience the hegemonic gender order differently than women and those assigned female at birth.[13] It is logical to gatekeepers of this social order if women and AFAB people wish to emulate masculinity, since masculinity is supposed to be superior to femininity. It is far less acceptable when AMAB people identify with femininity, since this opens up the possibility that masculinity is not in fact superior to femininity—an insinuation which threatens the entire patriarchal system.[14] Men and AMAB people who embrace femininity anyway, despite the stigma that is associated with it within this misogynistic cultural context, pay the price. Gatekeepers of the gender order penalize such deviance through social sanctioning and even threats, as Riley knows firsthand: "I can't just go outside wearing a dress and not have some verbal comment made to me, if not a threatening comment."

Indeed, several AMAB people in this sample cite fear as the dominant reason why they do not express their gender more freely. As Cleopatra explains, "You know, sometimes you find stuff, but you procrastinate dressing and presenting because of all the work added to what a typical woman would have to do, to put into it, of trying to get ready with their day. Of like all the mental preparedness you have to do for the day and how you fear what other people might say or do or your safety." These fears are founded: Cleopatra experiences regular harassment from strangers whenever they do muster the courage to express their femininity:

> I once wore a one-piece bathing suit because I wanted to express and I was very uncomfortable and unsure and obviously people looked at me and laughed at me. One time I wore a skirt and a blouse and lipstick and earrings to this night event at the hotel and I went on stage for this competition. And the guy was saying in Spanish all this stuff that was making fun of me to the whole audience and people were just laughing at me.

When people who were assigned male at birth express their femininity in a manner that is visually apparent, they are vulnerable to such episodes of harassment. In a risk–benefit analysis, AMAB people have more reasons than AFAB people to conceal their nonbinary gender and present as a man or to try to achieve unambiguous recognition as women. AMAB people remain more accountable to others within the gender binary system than AFAB people in this particular way.

Another key difference that emerged within these interviews involves money. The costs of "doing femininity" are considerably higher than the costs of "doing masculinity."[15] The idealized feminine aesthetic requires makeup, nail polish, hair products, and other products that are all subjected to the "pink tax." In addition, "women's clothes" are oftentimes more expensive than "men's clothes," and scrutinized much more harshly. As a result of these financial concerns, some AMAB people cannot afford to express themselves through feminized visual codes, as Mason explains: "The fact that most of my clothing is men's clothing makes it easier to do androgyny as a midpoint for right now, instead of, like, you know, having to buy a whole—a whole new wardrobe of women's clothing."

In certain cities, fashion standards render the cost of femininity even more staggering and prohibitive, as Avery discussed at length in their interview. Having moved from Georgia to New York City several years earlier, Avery reflected upon the differences between the cost of "doing femininity" in these two cultural fields: "Moving here, I've explored more ways to dress, but the problem is just money. You know? And I think one thing that people have to realize is that it's like very—it takes time to find yourself in this world. But also, sometimes, one of the reasons why people can't really do that is because they are constrained with financial issues." Avery notes that the fashion standards in New York City are much more stringent than those in Georgia, resulting in more pressure to buy expensive clothes. Fashionable women's clothes cost considerably more money than passable men's clothes; therefore, AFAB people may have an easier time shifting wardrobes (in some ways) than their AMAB counterparts. At the same time, nonbinary people are disproportionately impoverished compared to the general population.[16] Thus, the cost associated with "doing femininity" presents a significant and disproportionate obstacle for AMAB individuals who must save up sufficient funds in order to cultivate their desired aesthetics.

Race can also problematize people's ability to achieve social recognition as nonbinary, due to cultural stereotypes about what nonbinary or genderqueer people are supposed to look like.[17] As Kazi, who is Bengali, complains:

> I have had so many issues with the whole idea of what being genderqueer is. It's such a flexible term and people forget that, and people have this image of a genderqueer person as this skinny white androgynous person. Like, always skinny, white androgynous person. It's never a more feminine person or a masculine person. Sometimes people just think of a butch lesbian and that's it. That's it. But, it's not.

Those who happen to look like this stereotypical image of a genderqueer person may have an easier time being recognized as such, compared to those who present as more masculine or more feminine, or those who are simply not white. Dakota voices an awareness of this stereotype with discomfort because they recognize that they benefit from it: "The image that pops into my head when I hear of a nonbinary genderqueer is almost always skinny, white, AFAB. And I am essentially two of those and I know that has a certain cache and it sucks. And it's something that I try to think about and address where it's relevant." Dakota benefits from multiple axes of privilege that are interwoven within this genderqueer stereotype, though they are extremely uncomfortable with that situation. It is easier for them to achieve recognition as genderqueer or nonbinary and thus interactively "do" their gender, all by virtue of their genetics.

Another related issue that multiple people addressed in their interviews is "passing privilege," loosely defined as the tendency to be mistaken as cisgender by strangers. Those who benefit from "passing privilege" have a more difficult time achieving recognition as nonbinary and thereby redoing gender at the interactional level. They are also less likely to find themselves vulnerable to discrimination, compared to those who stand out as somehow visibly queer. As Kazi explains:

> There's a strange position I have as someone who can pass, so to speak. [...] I know I'm in a privileged position. I know I can hide myself a lot easier than some other trans folks and that's something I have to really think about. I have to know when my place is to step back as someone who is gender-neutral, genderqueer. I know that...I'm not pleased with it. I have my own issues where people don't recognize me.

Kazi feels like they should let others who are more visibly genderqueer represent their caucus. And yet, this is circular logic in some ways. Those who look like the stereotype are the ones who are more "visibly" genderqueer; if they are also the only people who are given the opportunity to represent genderqueer people as a group, then this reinforces the stereotype of what genderqueer people look like.

Race did not feature very strongly within discussions of gendered aesthetics among my interviewees, beyond these references to the white genderqueer stereotype. However, one noteworthy exception arose within my interview with Parker, who is Asian American. Parker speculates that their race might grant them more latitude regarding gender expression because Asian American men are stereotyped as being relatively feminine in the first place[18]:

> I think in general Asian American males are less stereotyped as hyper-masculine than any other race of males. So, I think that has made it a lot easier for me to accept my identity because there is less push-back against it, right? Because so many Asian Americans are allowed to be, and sometimes expected to be, more feminine than their White, Black, Latino, etc. colleagues. Then it made me less of a target, do you know what I mean?

Parker's feminine visual cues are not necessarily perceived as a sign of gender non-conformity or queerness; rather, these cues are perceived by others as a byproduct of racial difference. Parker believes that people are too distracted by their racial conspicuousness to notice their gender non-normativity within the majority white context of Long Island: "It's much more obvious, people can see me as Asian immediately. But it would take them a little bit longer to look at my fingernails or notice my socks are mismatched or see that, I don't know, I'm using hand gestures that are considered feminine or gay. That takes a little bit more to realize." Parker was not the only one to notice this racialized phenomenon. Jaylen also reported a similar observation about her (pronoun specified) experiences as a white person in a majority non-white environment:

> When I lived in Mozambique I was a teacher. So, every day I would go teach, I would wear pants and a button up shirt and no one really…sometimes my colleagues would, ya know, mention, "Why don't you ever wear a dress or a skirt?" But it was never, like—once again, in Mozambique my biggest problem was my foreignness, my Americanness, my whiteness. That was the weirdest thing about me. And the last thing on the list was that my Mozambican colleagues commented on the fact that I was kinda a little more masculine than usual.

Based on these anecdotes, it seems feasible that the salience of racial difference and gender difference is stronger in certain cultural contexts than in others. However, it is also quite possible that those who stand out due to their race feel even more pressure to conform to gender norms, since they function as group representatives; further research is necessary.

In addition to race and people's assigned sex, weather also affected people's ability to visually convey their nonbinary gender. Two AFAB people in my sample explained that it is more difficult to present a masculine appearance when hot weather requires them to wear fewer clothes and their bodies wind up on display. As Jesse explained: "You know what makes a big difference in my presentation is the heat. It's a lot easier to kind of dress in gender affirming ways when it's a little cooler. In the heat, it's a lot more difficult 'cause I just wanna wear dresses and shorts and stuff." Similarly, Marley deviates from their usual masculine presentation style during the hotter months, out of necessity: "People don't really know what to do with me because they see me presenting more masculine most of the time. Like, the summer is brutal for me. I'm very heat sensitive and I have no choice but to wear dresses or like, pass out in public so… Gender gets more complicated then."

Danger in the Public Sphere

Fairly obviously, the biggest consideration within field-contingent[19] outness revolves around safety considerations. Marley conceals their gender around their family "in order to just not get harassed." Similarly, Lisa does not display her gender if she knows that she will be visiting certain neighborhoods:

> I've been a little concerned about my neighborhood, sometimes at night. This is a Republican sort of neighborhood and there's a lot of—I've had a couple of incidents. It doesn't really stop me from doing what I do. But I try to schedule my trips on the subway, you know what I mean? At certain times of the day whether they—just any old time of the day. That is a particular thing that is going on with me in this particular neighborhood. There are certainly other neighborhoods in Brooklyn in which I would just not get dressed up in and go to.

Nonbinary people's access to spaces is limited by these safety concerns, especially on days when they are dressed in particularly unconventional ways. This omnipresent threat of violence is a perfect illustration of how nonbinary people find themselves held forcefully accountable to the gender binary system at the interpersonal level.

This threat intensifies when nonbinary people need to use the restroom in public. Considerable research has documented the violence and harassment that trans men and trans women encounter while trying to use public restrooms.[20] However, less research has focused explicitly on how nonbinary people navigate the gender binary system within these rigidly gendered spaces.[21] Whereas for trans men and trans women, there is one restroom that at least matches their gender identity, this is not the case for nonbinary people. Unless there is a gender-neutral option, nonbinary people must strategically select which gendered restroom to use, based not on their own gender identity, but on safety considerations.

This "restroom dilemma" is considerable for nonbinary people. Peyton has been physically chased out of both restrooms. As they elaborate:

> I've gone into the men's room, like, not even trying to look particularly feminine. And then cat-called out, like, "Who brought their girlfriend into the men's restroom?" And like, "What the fuck are you doing in here?" Like, "You took a wrong turn," And, of course, when people are calling you out in a restroom, you don't really wanna be there because you don't really know what's gonna go on. So, I would just turn around and leave. So, men's rooms, I never considered particularly safe. And then the same thing with women's rooms.

Women have asked me, like, "What the fuck are you doing in here?" Like, "You don't belong here, I can tell." Like, "I can see through that disguise."

Peyton has not experienced much difference in safety between the two gendered spaces; no matter which restroom they use, strangers hold them accountable to the gender binary by pressuring them to leave the space. Some of my interviewees have even literally been ushered into or out of a restroom by strangers who are eager to maintain order in their binary-gendered world. Cleopatra was shocked to experience this at a queer music venue in New York City:

I went with my two cis-female friends. I wanted to go to the bathroom. We went downstairs to the basement, wanting to use the women's bathroom, and there was a security guard, a woman, who kept shouting at me and telling me, "You should use the men's bathroom." And I said politely, "Under New York City law I can use the bathroom that I want," and then she kept shouting at me and said, "No, no. Get out of here. Men over there."

Even though they were in a queer venue, Cleopatra was ultimately held accountable to the gender binary system by the staff of that venue. Cleopatra tried to exercise their rights to use the restroom of their choice, but to no avail due to the establishment's binary gendered structure.

Justice encountered similar issues with gender binary enforcement at their school. Again, they held their ground and informed the staff about their rights, and in this case they had limited success: "I use whatever bathroom is available. I was confronted at school and told to no longer use the male bathroom. I told them they can't do that, I can use whichever one I identify with. And no one has stopped me since." Justice, like Cleopatra, had to confront a security guard about their rights when the guard took it upon himself to control which restroom they could use. In both of these anecdotes, the guards acted upon the belief that one can determine a person's gender based on their appearance. This common misunderstanding both illustrates and reflects the gender binary system's ideological conflation between sex, gender, and gender expression.

People who feel unsafe using gendered restrooms develop a number of strategies to protect themselves. For example, Jesse strategically selects a restroom on a case by case basis: "I will assess how safe I feel in the space and then decide which restroom to use." Meanwhile, others resolve this dilemma by refusing to use public restrooms at all, like Corey: "I usually hold it." Similarly, Alex says, "I don't use them. I go to the bathroom at home. I have a single stall bathroom at work that I use and I do not use public restrooms."

Others will use public restrooms if—and only if—they can confirm that no one else is using them. People's strategies for checking vary. Devin checks the restroom by themselves, while Lane solicits the help of friends: "If I'm with friends, then I usually ask them to check the toilets beforehand and give me a description on how everything looks." And finally, some interviewees explain that their decision is more circumstantial. For example, two interviewees specify that they will always default to the women's restroom in venues that serve alcohol, so as to avoid intoxicated men who may be especially prone to homophobic/transphobic violence. This strategy revolves around the assumption that women will not physically act upon their homophobia/transphobia, even if intoxicated.

In effect, gendered restrooms function as physical manifestations of the gender binary in the public sphere. Nonbinary people must regularly choose between two rigidly gendered boxes, neither of which fit, under the surveillance of strangers. When they finally choose one out of necessity, they risk confrontations with self-appointed gender-police, who protect the gender binary by expelling anyone who does not fit. Sometimes nonbinary people are even held accountable to the gender binary by literal police and security guards, as noted above, who abuse their power to monitor the boundaries of gendered restrooms.

The public restroom provides the most concrete example of the dangers of nonbinary recognition/misrecognition in the public sphere, but such danger is not confined to those rigidly gendered spaces. Three people also recounted episodes of harassment while in transit, either on foot or in public transportation systems. These confrontational moments can be extremely frightening, especially if the nonbinary person is traveling alone. For example, Marley was harassed on the subway by an intoxicated man who repeatedly referred to them as a "he-she":

> I was coming back from my outreach program so I was binding. I was wearing a button-down shirt and a jacket, and a man and his girlfriend got on the subway. They were both on some sort of substance. Whether they were drunk or high, I don't know. He was looking to pick fights and he spent about five minutes standing in front of me, like, holding onto the rail, looking down at me and talking about how uncomfortable the he-she was, sitting in front of him, and how it must be getting very upset. For about five minutes, very loudly, on a crowded train. No one did anything. He eventually sat down next to the woman next to me and started harassing her instead.

Marley was saddened to note that none of the passengers in the subway car intervened while witnessing this moment of public harassment. Through their silence, the other strangers tacitly endorsed this man's decision to accost Marley for deviating from binary gendered ideals. Marley further notes that these incidents have been on the rise: "Recently I've been getting harassed more, both on the subway and in public and with bathrooms and… that's less than pleasant. But I kind of have to look at it as it comes with the territory." Marley constructs harassment as an inevitability while presenting their nonbinary gender in the public sphere.

Like Marley, Cleopatra also experiences heightened vulnerability toward gender-based harassment on the subway:

> I feel like when I'm like dressing more feminine, I have a lot of men who make fun of me and try to cat-call me, but in a more mocking way, you know? And I definitely feel uncomfortable. I remember one year I was on the train at night. There was, like, seven guys who hobbled around me and they're, like, "Hey, mami! What's going on?" or whatever. And I knew it wasn't, like, "Oh, me being desired!" It was me being joked on and made fun of and I felt very uncomfortable and unsafe.

Cleopatra, who is openly transfeminine, frequently endures mocking cat-calls from men. They note that the seemingly sexual attention they attract from these men is not sincere, but rather thinly veiled expressions of transphobia and homophobia. This type of recognition from men functions as a tacit warning that their conspicuousness is an invitation for sexualized and gendered violence. The implication is that if they want to look like a woman, they better be prepared to be treated like a woman—which in rape culture insinuates violence.

When I asked Lisa whether she had ever experienced any sort of discrimination or harassment for her gender expression, she replied, "The most recent one was not that long ago in the entryway of my building here in New York. It scared me, but they actually were not—they were kids. Which bothers me." Lisa went on to enumerate several strategies that she has developed in order to decrease the risk of such confrontations by self-appointed members of the gender-police:

> You know, I keep going. I've never been beat up or kicked or engaged with people when they show distain for me. I don't do anything, you know? I go completely the opposite direction. If it's at night, I'll move into a lighted store or somewhere. I do not engage in anything like that. If it's on the subway, I find what car the conductor is in, I go there and talk to them. I just do not engage with any sort of distain or disapproval or jokes or anything, you know?

Lisa recounts this episode of gender-based harassment with surprise, citing her avoidance of situations that could put her in danger. However, no matter how many strategies Lisa utilizes to minimize danger, she cannot avoid interacting with strangers altogether. In this case, danger was waiting for her on her very doorstep, perpetrated by the least likely suspects—children. This anecdote illustrates a few important points. First of all, people are indoctrinated into binary gender ideology from a young age. In this case, children took it upon themselves to hold a sixty-year old accountable to binary gender ideals. Second, no one can ever fully escape the gender binary's accountability structures.

Conclusion

The aim of this chapter was to highlight the various ways in which nonbinary people try to escape misgendering from strangers and associates. Some announce their gender verbally, either by stating "I am nonbinary" or through "they/them/their" pronoun declarations. Some assert it through visual cues, as they attempt to look less like a man or a woman. All of these practices, be they verbal or visual, require effort on the part of the nonbinary person. This labor is never-ending and ultimately exhausting. Due to the common erroneous assumption that everyone is either a man or a woman, it is considered impolite to admit confusion about a person's gender or to ask for clarification. Instead, people take their best guess of these two binary options and move on with the interaction—unless otherwise corrected. A few of my interviewees take it upon themselves to correct strangers who do this, but many just let it go due to the fleeting nature of the interaction. It would simply require too much of their limited energy to set the record straight.

Some of my interviewees expect strangers to shift their manner of interpersonal interaction in recognition of their nonbinary gender. However, recognition by strangers is clearly not always a desirable outcome. These harassment episodes illustrate how "interpersonal accountability" functions in daily life to effectively maintain the gender status quo. Of course, "interpersonal accountability" also manifests through misrecognition when friends, family, and significant others fail or refuse to affirm the nonbinary person's gender. But even those who are blessed with an accepting inner circle remain accountable to the gender binary system in the public sphere. When strangers recognize the nonbinary person as someone who does not belong in "men's" or "women's" spaces—or in the public sphere at all—some take it upon themselves to socially sanction the deviant person and effectively erase their existence through expulsion or worse. Although certain cultural arenas register to my interviewees as relatively safe spaces, the public sphere at large is still not constructed as such.

I hope my cisgender readers will read between the lines here and understand that they likely have met nonbinary people before. In fact, they have likely met *many* nonbinary people before, many more than they realize. They simply did not know it because the nonbinary person (or people) decided to let the misgendering go uncorrected. Nonbinary people typically do clarify their gender when interacting with strangers whom they perceive to be knowledgeable about queer issues, but otherwise they carefully consider whether the disclosure is sufficiently worthwhile and safe. If no one has told you before that they are nonbinary, it may be necessary to adjust the cues that you are broadcasting. Make sure that it is common knowledge that you are an LGBTQ ally, maybe even announce your own pronoun when you introduce yourself to people, and you might be surprised how many nonbinary people announce themselves right back to you.

Notes

1. Gimlin (2002).
2. For more on "femmephobia," see Blair and Hoskin (2015), Hoskin (2019), and Blair and Hoskin (2016).
3. For more on nonbinary people's experiences with drag, see Rogers (2018) "Drag as a Resource: Trans* and Nonbinary Individuals in the Southeastern United States."
4. Synnott (1987) and Friedman (2013).
5. Synnott (1987).
6. Synnott (1987) and Weitz (2011).
7. Thompson (2009), Tate (2007), Ndichu and Upadhyaya (2019), Craig (2002), and Caldwell (2003).
8. Pfeffer (2014).
9. Basow (1992), Darwin (2017), Fahs (2011), Herzig (2015), Tiggemann and Hodgson (2008), Toerien et al. (2005).
10. For more on the association between women's body hair and feminism, see Herzig (2015) *Plucked: A History of Hair Removal* and Darwin (2017) "The Pariah Femininity Hierarchy: Comparing White Women's Body Hair and Fat Stigmas in the United States.".
11. Connell (1987).
12. See Westbrook and Schilt (2014).
13. R.W. Connell (1987, 1995), Schippers (2007), and Budgeon (2014).
14. R.W. Connell (1987, 1995).

15. Duesterhaus et al. (2011).
16. Harrison-Quintana et al. (2012).
17. Davidson (2007).
18. Lu and Wong (2013).
19. By "field-contingent," I mean that people are "out" in certain groups or spaces but not in others. Cultural sociologists sometimes refer to these discrete pockets of society as "fields".
20. Overall (2007), Doan (2010), Browne (2004), Devor (1989), Halberstam (1998), and Cavanagh (2011).
21. For other research on nonbinary people and restroom use, see Dubin et al. (2021) and Barbee and Schrock (2019).

Redoing Relationships

"There's two different kinds of transition. There's social transition and medical transition. And social transition is definitely a process that's in place with being more open about the fact that I identify as gender neutral and using 'they' pronouns. And slowly but surely, getting more people to refer to me in terms of neutral 'they/them/their' as opposed to 'she/her/woman,' etc.... That is a transition that's in process. Probably will be for the rest of my life" (Sydney). Sydney is a white 32-year old from North Carolina who has "come out" multiple times—first as a lesbian and later as nonbinary. Although they have not pursued surgical procedures or hormone replacement therapy, they have still gone through a significant transitioning process since disclosing their nonbinary gender to people in their life. Medical transitions are not the only type of transition.

The focus of this chapter is on this other type of transition that they describe, which they call a "social transition." Whereas the first stage of "redoing gender" requires people to rethink sex and gender, this next stage requires a much more interactional process, which I call "redoing relationships." This chapter will illustrate how nonbinary people redo their relationships with their parents, siblings, friends, romantic partners, and children. How do they achieve recognition as nonbinary, when others are so accustomed to the notion that they are men or women? What types of obstacles do they encounter and how do they resolve these challenges? These are the central questions of this chapter.

H. Darwin, *Redoing Gender*, https://doi.org/10.1007/978-3-030-83617-7_5

Again, the experience of social transitioning is not unique to the nonbinary population. All trans people go through some sort of social transition and experience a range of reactions from their family members who are invested in the concept of them as a daughter/son/sister/brother/boyfriend/girlfriend/mother/father. The relationship must shift if it is going to continue. The family member must adopt a different "relationship script"[1] and use gender-affirming terminology for the person, whether they are a trans man/trans woman or nonbinary. The key distinction is that family members of the former can trade one binary relational script for another. Family members of the latter must be receptive to adopting a relational script that they have likely never used before.

Not everyone in my sample had gone through a social transition at the time of our initial interview. Some had only very recently discovered their nonbinary gender and had yet to disclose it to other people in their lives. However, the majority of my interviewees *had* begun to disclose their gender and pronouns to others, and coach their loved ones through the requisite "relational shift" away from binary-inflected terminology and mannerisms.

I conceptualize this social transitioning process not in terms of "coming out" terminology, but in terms of the various forms of labor that it requires. While gay and lesbian people primarily perform declarative labor ("I am gay") while "coming out," nonbinary people must do much more than verbally declare themselves nonbinary. Following the disclosure, they frequently must also explain what nonbinary gender means, coach people through etiquette (such as terminology), remind people when they forget, and perform emotional labor while loved ones struggle to let go of their old concept of them. Perhaps unfairly, the burden is on nonbinary people to coach their loved ones through this transition, a process which is often uncomfortable—if not overtly painful—for both parties. Social transitioning requires a careful balance between identity management concerns (i.e., "coming out" and achieving social recognition) and exhaustion management concerns (i.e., "burnout").

Parents

Kennedy is a white 21-year-old Jewish college student in the Pacific Northwest, with curly short-cropped brown hair and warm brown eyes. I knew Kennedy's mother through a liberal Jewish synagogue we had attended together when I was an undergraduate college student. When Kennedy's mother saw my call for respondents on Facebook, she encouraged them to respond. It was a little unclear whether Kennedy participated in the interview because they genuinely wanted to, or whether they had only done so to please their mother. While answering my questions, they were also texting, typing on their computer, playing with their hair, leaning back and sighing, stretching, and often losing their train of thought.

According to Kennedy, their mother was not so great about respecting their gender at first. Kennedy's parents apparently didn't "get it" until Kennedy finally reached a breaking point:

> It took them awhile and took me sort of like, not being willing to talk to them, ignore them, and avoid them for quite a while for them to understand. And then my mom and I started to kinda have a big screaming match for them to sort of understand the gravity of the situation of like…like, it really hurts me a lot when you misgender me and won't apologize, like, won't make an effort and correct yourself. And since then it's been good.

Both of Kennedy's parents have become more receptive to their gender over time, ever since Kennedy managed to impress upon them how much misgendering hurt them. Kennedy has had to engage in some coaching and corrective labor, but their parents also take the initiative to ask questions and research or innovate gender-neutral terminology as replacements for binary-gendered terms—both in English and in Hebrew. All in all, their parents have been receptive toward their gender and willing to redo their relationship in a more gender-affirming way.

Lane's mother had quite a different reaction. Lane is a white 24-year old from the Soviet Union who was living in Denmark at the time of this interview. They had a relatively expressionless affect throughout our interview, but seemed perfectly comfortable discussing their mother's hurtful reaction toward their gender: "She had a couple of mental breakdowns because of it, when I came out to her as trans, like, the days afterwards she would get spontaneous nose blood and she had to call in sick from work. That's like… that's how badly she felt about it." Instead of taking this personally, Lane is willing to attribute at least some of this reaction to cultural differences: "She grew up in the Soviet Union where gay people were put in prison for being gay. So, the whole trans thing, it's like a whole new level of weird, I guess. I'm just, like, completely shaking her foundation, her worldview or whatever." Lane waited patiently for their mother to process her emotions and signal that she was ready to move forward with their relationship in a more gender-affirming way: "It took almost two years before it started getting better because she was not using the right pronouns or anything. But at least she's trying to not use gendered terms. Instead of 'daughter,' she uses 'my child' for example."

Addison, a white 26-year-old Quaker from Chicago, also had to endure some painful emotions from their mother during their social transition:

> My mother, especially within the past couple of years, has sort of gone through what she described as a mourning period for losing her daughter, so to speak. And not to say that she doesn't love me or doesn't talk to me, or anything like that. We're still close, it's just she has come to terms in her own way with the fact that I don't identify as female. And that is a loss for her, I think, because for her gender is important. And it does shape how she interacts with people and she feels closer to women than she does for men in certain ways. We had a lot of different conversations about that and they've all kind of sucked.

Addison's mother acknowledges their child's nonbinary gender, but makes it very clear that this transition has robbed them of something precious—the ability to interact with them as a daughter. This sense of loss was a common theme when interviewees recounted their parents' initial reactions, especially if they were the only child of their assigned sex/gender within the family unit. Again, this type of reaction is not specific to nonbinary gender disclosures, but also reported by trans men and trans women elsewhere.[2]

Although Kennedy, Lane, and Addison have endured some pain while redoing their relationships with their parents, they did eventually arrive at a point of achieving gender recognition. This is not the case for everyone, however. Several people in my sample encountered hostility and malicious misgendering from their parents long after they disclosed their gender. Corey, for example, has resigned themselves to the fact that they simply cannot "do" their gender in their relationship with their resistant parents: "I get a lot of micro-aggressions from my parents because they are not supportive and they will not use the right name or the right pronouns for me. My father even went to the level to say that he will never, ever use 'they' for me. Because he doesn't get it." Even though Corey had started to physically transition at the time of this interview, they remain unable to socially transition within their family unit. In a slightly different way, Morgan's mother also refuses to acknowledge their nonbinary gender as legitimate: "She was like, 'No, you're 100% female. Like, 'You're a woman because you have a vagina' and all that stuff. It was like, 'According to Masters and Johnson, you're female.'" Morgan's mother insists upon her right to misgender them by invoking biologically essentialist logic (that reduces gender to genitalia). As Corey and Morgan's experiences indicate, a nonbinary person's desire to redo a relationship is simply not enough unto itself to make it happen. The other person must also be receptive to the shift and willing to rethink sex and gender. If they are not receptive, the relationship inevitably falters.

Of course, some parents have been extremely receptive to their children's nonbinary gender disclosure. K, a white 30-year old, was pregnant with their first child at the time of our interview and experiencing lots of thoughts about nonbinary parenting. K has been "out" as nonbinary for five years, uses "them/them/their pronouns," and is considering a medical transition once they are finished "chest-feeding" their infant. K's father is one of the most proactively supportive parents in this sample, in that he invited the disclosure in the first place, based on a hunch: "He was like, 'Hey, I learned some stuff and I just wanted to see if this applied to you in some way that I had missed' and so I really appreciated that, cause he figured it out without me having to tell him. I was still working out how to tell him at that point." This isn't to say that K's father is perfect, but he has proven enthusiastically receptive to change: "He still messes up every once in awhile and says 'she,' but if he does, he apologizes. He actually asked me at Christmas when we were visiting family, he was like, 'So does this whole pregnancy thing, like, are you going to be ok being called Mom? Like, what do you want me to call you to the kid?'" K's father had obviously already gone through the process of rethinking sex and gender before these interactions even happened. K is deeply appreciative of his proactive support of them.

Although K's father is exceptionally receptive to nonbinary gender, he is not the only extremely supportive parent in this sample. Reagan's mother has also been proactively supportive from the very beginning:

> After a Lipstick Lesbian Awareness party, I called my mom. And I was like, "I think I'm genderqueer. I don't know what I am, but I'm not a woman." And I was crying and she was like, "Okay, we'll figure it out, I just don't want you to be sad." Because for the twenty years that I was in the closet, I was so sad and depressed and my mom, once I came out to her, was really upset that I thought I couldn't trust her. I decided that, like, keeping that kind of secret inside was eating me alive. And so, when I figured out this next part of my journey or my identity I was very open about it immediately and was like, I need support, I need help, I want my family to be on board.

Reagan's mother had already made it clear to them that they wanted to support them, no matter how their identity changed over time. Because they knew their mother would be receptive, they were able to begin to redo that relationship as soon as they had their epiphany that they were not a woman. Reagan's father has struggled a little more with their social transition, but Reagan gratefully acknowledges that at least he is trying:

My dad likes to write me letters, which is cute, but he always puts "Miss" or "Lisa" on the envelopes. And I was like, "Dad, I really need you to hear me when I'm saying I don't wanna go by Lisa. And using the word 'Miss' is implying something that I don't identify with, and it's hurtful and it makes me feel sad when I see it." And it's taking him…awhile. But, I just got a letter from him yesterday and it said "Reagan." So, I was like "Alright, we're making progress.

Reagan's father has good intentions, even if his linguistic transition to using gender-neutral terminology for Reagan has been imperfect. At the end of the day, Reagan is heartened to know that the relational shift is in progress and they try to remain patient while coaching him through the adjustment.

Siblings

Parents are not the only ones who have to redo their relationship with a nonbinary person after their gender disclosure; siblings also have to make adjustments in the terminology and relational scripts that they habitually use. Siblings did not come up nearly as often as parents in the interviews, but a handful of people mentioned this relational shift as a struggle. For example, Reagan's sister had a particularly difficult time with their transition: "My sister broke down one time and was just like, 'We're all struggling so much and we don't know what to do. We're losing our sister, our daughter, and I know you're the same person. But, again, it's those words that we're getting caught up on." Reagan felt obligated to provide emotional support to their sister following this conversation, an additional form of labor on top of the coaching that they were already providing for their family members. They feel badly that their transition is causing their sister so much emotional pain, but not badly enough to accept misgendering. They still need her to continue forward in the redoing of their sibling dynamic.

Donna's sister has also proven to be invested in the concept of having a sister, but Donna does not mind. Donna, a white 28-year old from Norway, moved to Minneapolis to be with their child's other transgender parent, from whom they later separated. Donna is no longer in touch with their parents, but they have tried to maintain a relationship with their sister throughout their transition:

We're not actually twins, but we call each other twin. And like, we always say "sister bonding," or "sisterly bonding." Or you know, just lots of things with the word sister in it. Our brother "sisterly bonds" with us as well, so it's not like, we don't hold fast to it. But she's like, "Can we still have 'sisterly bonding?'" I'm like, "Duh, of course we can." And you know, it's—but, it's still hard for her. My parents are always like, "It's the two girls and Mike," or whatever. It's honestly the language that's tripping everyone up. I think it's probably the hardest part.

Like Reagan's sister, Donna's sister feels certain that the language is "tripping everyone up." Unlike Reagan, however, Donna does not expect their sister to stop calling them "sister." It means more to their sister to hold onto the terminology than it means for Donna to leave the label behind. Clearly, different nonbinary people have different expectations of their siblings during their social transition.

Children

People ultimately have limited control over whether strangers, parents, partners, or siblings remember to use the correct language while addressing them, but they are able to exercise some agency over how their children address them. Three people in my sample are parents, one was pregnant during the interview, and another was actively pursuing impregnation.

Dakota, a white 31-year-old high school teacher in the Bay Area with wavy shoulder-length brown hair, thick eyebrows, and fair skin, has felt increasing discomfort with their designated "father" label in recent years: "I've started being more proactive about pronouns in the last two or three years, mostly because I hadn't quite before felt an unpleasantness around the word father and that parenting role. And I realized that I needed to articulate this in a wider way for people to understand." At the time of this interview, Dakota's child was four. They have made a concerted effort to switch over to using gender-neutral labels such as "parent" with their child, and correspondingly refer to their child as such instead of as their "son." However, Dakota clarified with clear ambivalence that they still use masculine pronouns for him. "I feel kind of awkward having assigned my child a gender despite having some feelings about coercive gender full stop. It takes a village, and most of our village is, like, 'Oh, this child has external genitalia and therefore is a he.'" Dakota feels conflicted about openly endorsing gender fluidity in their child, as a queer parent who is under constant surveillance by the cisgender people around them:

A lot of my in-laws feel like because 10% of the clothes that he owns are pink, that is evidence of the fact that we are forcing pink on him. Although he will frequently say that pink is his favorite color, he will also say that about a lot of other colors. That's frustrating. I feel like that isn't something we would be dealing with if we were an entirely typical straight couple. There would be a lot more clapping, like, "Oh, that's brave of you!" But because we are who we are, we are put to a level of "Don't indoctrinate."

If Dakota didn't feel so accountable to others' appraisals of their parenting skills, they would possibly encourage more gender experimentation in their child. As it stands, they toe the line between their ideal parenting experience and what feels safe.

Dakota's fears are unfortunately founded. Sam, another parent in this sample, has had Child Protective Services called on them twice by neighbors for no justifiable reason. Thankfully, both times the charges were dropped straightaway. "I dislike being judged immediately just on my presentation as someone who is not trustworthy as a parent. [...] Even on my most relaxed days, I'm always aware at least in the very back of my mind there are definitely people out there who are watching everything I do and hoping for me to fail." Sam conceived their child on their own ten years ago. When I asked them to clarify, they explained "It was an intentional pregnancy. I mean, it's kind of hard to *not* have an intentional pregnancy when you don't typically sleep with men..." Sam experiences some frustration when other people do not respect or recognize their parent role in relation to their daughter: "I've had people be like, 'Oh, well, it's really nice of your friend to take you out shopping' to my daughter. Or 'your aunt,' or you know, 'your uncle' or 'whoever this person is' you know. I'm most of the time assumed that I am not her parent [chuckle]. And we laugh about it, she kind of rolls with it, takes it you know, okay... But once in a while it kind of irritates me." As it happens, Sam is not a "mom" or a dad": "I'm 'Moda,' which is 'mo' for mom and 'd-a' for dad, it's both." Arguably, Sam's biggest obstacle in the parenting role as a nonbinary person has been society's resistance to them in this role.

K was pregnant at the time of this interview and beginning to think about how to "do" their nonbinary gender in relation to their child. K voiced a desire for an innovative parenting term such as Sam's "moda," but hadn't found one that resonated with them:

It's just me and a relationship between me and my body and me and the kid. I think I'm ok being called "mom" by the kid, but I think it will feel weird being called "mom" by other people. But I don't really know how to navigate that yet because there's not really, like, "parents"...but like, I don't know. I want there to be a word. I don't want to be like, "Just call me by my name, child."

Beyond the labeling dilemma, K had not given much thought to the various challenges of nonbinary parenting.

Donna similarly uses the "mother" label with some ambivalence, simply because it is what their gender-neutral child got used to calling them before Donna realized that they were nonbinary. Donna (who is from Norway) and their American ex got married after having their child, for the ease of continuing the relationship, given immigration laws. The relationship ended after Donna moved to Minneapolis to be with their ex, but they continue to share custody and reside near one another. Throughout the course of their relationship, both partners' genders changed considerably, though in very different ways. Their different relationships with the gender binary contributed to their different perspectives on childrearing and on relating to their child:

> In the past, my ex has identified very strongly within the binary, and seeing it all as you know a binary thing. And so whenever our kid expressed the wish to wear dresses, my ex would very much sort of actively encourage she/her pronouns, and call our kid a girl, like exclusively. And, sort of ignoring the times when they would say, "Oh, I wanna be a boy today" [laughs], you know. So that has been a little bit challenging, trying to have conversations where I want to respect her view and how she feels about her own gender identity, but also making clear that to me there's more than that.

Donna and their ex send their child to a queer-friendly private school. Thus, their surrounding community is supportive—the primary issue is that the parents project very different gender ideologies and experiences upon their child.

The process of "redoing relationships" between nonbinary people and their loved ones is tricky, to say the least. Nonbinary people expect to have their gender recognized after disclosing it to others, which requires some reprogramming on other people's part. Those who have always taken the gender binary for granted must suddenly rethink sex and gender, their linguistic habits, and their ways of relating to other people. Not everyone is willing to invest energy and effort into making this relational shift happen, however, and even those who *are* receptive toward the relational shift oftentimes require additional labor from the nonbinary person—such as explanations, coaching, and emotional support. Thus, the decision to "come out" to family members is one that nonbinary people do not take lightly.

Sexual/Romantic Partners

Family members are not the only people who are intimately affected by a nonbinary gender disclosure. Romantic and sexual partners are also deeply implicated and expected to engage in their own relational shift as they redo sexuality as well as redo the relationship more broadly. Partners' responses vary widely, with some proving less willing to redo their sexual relationship than others. Perhaps unsurprisingly, those who are invested in sexuality scripts that revolve around binary gendering encounter greater difficulty during this transition than those who are more sexually fluid.

Again, before this redoing of sexuality can even begin, nonbinary people must often *rethink* their sexuality in light of their gender identity. If someone identified as a lesbian before realizing they were nonbinary, for example, they have to seriously consider how they feel about continuing to claim that label. As Rhiannon explains, "Discovering nonbinary identities at the same time that I was thinking about my sexuality kind of helped me come to terms with, like, 'Lesbian doesn't really fit me.' Because I'm not really a girl who loves girls. I'm a nonbinary person who likes girls and other nonbinary people." Sexuality labels can matter a great deal to others—for example, some lesbians exclusively date other lesbians. Labels can also matter quite a lot to nonbinary people themselves, as continued partnership with a self-identified lesbian might make someone who was assigned female at birth feel misgendered, as River separately explained:

> Once I came to that terminology, like, I wouldn't be comfortable or find it possible to be coupled with someone who is a cis man, who identifies as straight or a cis woman who identifies as a lesbian. And I had that with a prior partner where that person identified as a lesbian at the time, who I think now identifies as also nonbinary and queer rather than as lesbian. But I was like, you know, for me I find it invalidating to my sexuality to be coupled that way.

Evidently, sexual orientation labels wield the potential to affirm or invalidate a person's nonbinary gender. Not surprisingly, most people in my sample who identified as gay, lesbian, or straight before realizing they were nonbinary have since changed their label to queer, bisexual, or pansexual to better reflect their gender. Other labels that people in my sample use include androsexual, asexual, gynesexual, nonbinary lesbian, gynephilic, panromantic, demisexual, and graysexual.

K uses the queer label to convey their apathy toward other people's gender: "It's an umbrella term for like a shrug because it's sort of everything. I mean, I've dated dudes, women, couple of trans dudes, couple of nonbinary people...." Meanwhile, Hunter uses the queer label as a shorthand way to communicate that both their gender and sexuality are queer: "For me, I'm bisexual as well as being genderqueer, so I just identify as queer. I should probably just get a big shirt that says 'Hey, I'm queer.' Because that encompasses all of it. It fits under sexuality, whatever." Hunter came out as bi in seventh grade, but at this point they prefer to simply use the label "queer," in part due to the stigmas associated with bisexuality and pansexuality: "It's hard for me to say that I'm genderqueer and pansexual because people are like, 'Oh, you're just really trying to be everything.' There are some people within the community that look at me and they're like, 'Oh, really, ok, you're one of them.'" Here, Hunter refers to the dismissive assumption that bisexual people are simply experimenting or transitioning from straight to gay.[3] Similarly, some assume that nonbinary people are either experimental cis people or passing through the identity on the way to becoming a trans man or a trans woman.

Kennedy identifies as gay and as gynephillic, which they define as a sexual preference for people with vaginas: "I generally am attracted to people with certain configuration of body parts but I don't care what their gender is." When asked how they understand the meaning of the gay label, in light of their nonbinary gender, Kennedy mused:

> What even is gay? In one sense, the word refers to a man who is attracted to other men. But gay is also just sort of used as a general term for queerness, like queer and gay. And if I'm not in the gender binary, then I'm clearly not straight, because to be straight... Straightness implies you are one binary gender and you are attracted to the other. If I'm not straight, then, well.... What are people that aren't straight? They are gay.

Kennedy understands everyone to share some overlap in gender with them, leading them to conclude that any relationship they are in is automatically a gay relationship: "Anybody who is attracted to me is gay. I'm not a gender that they are and so... like, I'm not the opposite gender, so..." Kennedy does not bother to disclose their gender to others during one-time hookups, but if it seems like the relationship might lead somewhere, they make a point to have this conversation. "If I'm gonna be dating someone, they have to be, like, not shitty about gender stuff. And then if they are gonna be not shitty then they probably won't have a problem with me, like, being silly, and being like, 'Well, you are gay now because you are attracted to me. Woops!'".

River also identifies as gay, but has operationalized the meaning of this term quite differently: "I refer to myself as double gay, in sort of a joking way. Like, I'm sort of masculine of center or androgynous and the people I'm attracted to generally fall under that heading." River went on to explain, "I feel like, you know, there's people who are gay or queer who are attracted to people who present oppositely? Or [chuckle]—in an opposite way from themselves, and then there are people who, you know, tend to be attracted to people who present similarly to themselves."

Lisa also has complicated feelings toward the gay label, since her partnership started as a presumably gay relationship. Identifying as gay makes Lisa feel misgendered, though, as it is a label that she claimed before her gender transition. She hesitantly confided that the more feminine she becomes, the more straight her relationship feels:

> And it's almost—I don't even know if I can say it, because I'm so conditioned not to say it—but it feels straight. I mean, it does. I'm being really honest with you. I get a whole bunch of shit for that. It's only now that I'm beginning to understand my own sexual responses towards men and it's not a gay thing, it's really not. It's more of a female thing. So, I guess it's more of a straight thing than it is gay.

Lisa was intimately involved with the gay community before her transition, but the label simply does not reflect her gendered experience of her sexuality any longer. Lisa was pleasantly surprised by her partner's willingness to redo his sexuality when Lisa finally disclosed her nonbinary gender to him:

> That was what was so great about meeting my husband. He actually met me when I was binary male and as I realized that I did not want to be binary male, he's been there right along with me the whole way. Never once lessening his sexual attraction for me or never once pushing me aside or anything, you know? So, I think it's about being really clear about who you are, and making sure the other person knows that you know who you are. And then they can make decisions about it. Some people—their sexual attraction to other people is purely physical. And sometimes it's physical and emotional, sometimes it's purely an emotional/spiritual thing. I think, luckily for me and my particular relationship, we have all of it. He's gone with me through the transition and is still here.

Lisa considers herself lucky that her husband was attracted to her as a person and not as a gay man. Lisa's husband was willing and able to make the transition to a different type of relationship as his partner embraced her nonbinary gender.

Addison's partner has also been unconditionally gender-affirming since the beginning of their relationship when he asked them to clarify their pronouns. They frequently discuss gender and sexual attraction, running a number of theoretical scenarios by one another: "We think about this a lot, in terms of 'Would you really be attracted to me if I was like in this different body, but still myself?' But they've been fruitful and obviously we're still together, so I think it's been really good for both of us to be constantly questioning where our desires come from." Crucial to the success of this relationship is their partner's ongoing willingness to question where his desires come from, as well as his receptivity to the possibility that his partner's gender and/or body might change again in the future. This supportive dynamic is dependent upon an open line of communication between the two partners and a mutual embrace of gender and sexual fluidity.

As mentioned earlier, this type of relational shift might be easier for those who are less invested in rigidly defined gender roles or sexual scripts. For example, K's long-term partner is willing to follow whatever script they want: "I've been with a cis-dude for like 7 years. And he's totally fine with all of my gender things, you know. He would call me his boyfriend if I wanted him to. Neither of us are very straight, so he gets it." K's partner is completely flexible about their relational style and their sexuality. K attributes this flexibility to their partner's own queer sexuality, which is neither defined nor compromised by K's gender. He is supportive of his partner's gender journey wherever it might take them.

A few people stipulate that their partners are supportive of their nonbinary gender identity on an abstract level, but that the sexual relationship might become compromised if they decided to pursue physical changes. For example, Ashton knows for a fact that their partner's support is contingent upon their body remaining the same:

> I kind of jokingly said, "What if I was a trans man and wanted to transition surgically?" And his answer at that time was like, "I don't think I could stay with you because you're a whole different situation than what I bargained for in the beginning." But, I became nonbinary and don't have any surgical plans, so…I guess he's fine with that.

Even though they joke about it, Ashton understands that their relationship might terminate if they pursue surgery or even hormones. At this point in time, they do not have any desire to physically transition, so this caveat is a nonissue. However, the knowledge that their partner feels so strongly about their body causes Ashton to wonder whether he really recognizes them as nonbinary at all.

Unfortunately, some partners are not just unsupportive, but actively abusive in their refusal to recognize their partner's nonbinary gender. As Kazi shares, "I've had tense—with that one person who I had to be extremely feminine for. I cannot put even a gentle dent in their heterosexuality. They were terrified and I had to go backwards." In their relationship with a cisgender man, Kazi found themselves pressured to perform femininity, as though they still identified as a cisgender woman. To do otherwise would have threatened their partner's sense of self as heterosexual. Similarly, Sydney's cisgender male partner continued to misgender Sydney following their nonbinary gender disclosure:

> I tried opening up to him, as I was being like, "You know, I don't think I identify as a woman" and that threatened him a lot. He always either tried to change the subject, tried to be like, "Oh! You know, I still see you as a woman!" Like, it was supposed to be reassuring to me or something. [...] You know, he had a very—he was not just straight, but he had a very hyper-masculine identity and fancied himself a bit of a ladies' man. And couldn't... you know, he could not see himself being with not a woman. He didn't want to leave me, but his solution was to continue misgendering me. And that sucked.

Sydney, like Kazi, suspected that their cisgender male partner's refusal to recognize their nonbinary gender reflected their investment in maintaining a heterosexual identity. These men were not willing to redo their sexuality in recognition of their partners' nonbinary gender; instead, they invalidated their partner's gender in preservation of their own (hetero)sexuality.

It is not just heterosexual cis men who struggle to recognize their partners' nonbinary gender. Respondents share anecdotes about being pressured to present as more masculine or more feminine by queer partners as well, so as to preserve their own relational sense of self. For example, Marley tearfully recollected memories of an abusive fiancé who refused to recognize the validity of their nonbinary gender:

> I was engaged to a somewhat abusive partner during this process, who was out as genderqueer. And they felt like they had a monopoly on identity and that it was their thing, and I couldn't also have feelings about gender. And part of their dysphoria was very aggressively gendering me female [...] A lot of their dysphoria rides on the fact that they could not impregnate me. Like, wanting us to be read as heterosexual when we were out. Like, pushing me towards the more femme side of the spectrum in order to make themselves feel better about their gender.

Like Sydney and Kazi, Marley was pressured to present in a more feminine manner in order to fulfill their partner's gendered sexuality. Marley's partner effectively held them accountable to binary gender ideals through this pressure.

As these stories illustrate, when a nonbinary person discloses their gender to a significant other, the disclosure has a direct impact on the relationship, as well as on the partner's sexuality. Some partners are aware of the person's nonbinary gender from the beginning of the relationship, but others must undergo a significant relational shift after the relationship has already begun. This relational shift can require a "redoing"[4] of the partner's sexuality, which they are not always able or willing to perform. If they are unable to make this change, the relationship inevitably ends.

Friends

In addition to family members and significant others, friends must also change the way that they relate to a nonbinary person in order to demonstrate that they support and recognize the person's gender. The Internet makes it easier for people to publicize their nonbinary gender to all of their friends and associates at once, and notionally avoid misgendering and/or a never-ending series of one-on-one "coming out" interactions. However, the disjuncture between online and offline realities can produce awkward experiences for nonbinary people, as Jesse explains:

> I post a lot of queer stuff on Facebook and a lot of trans stuff on Facebook. I'll just be like, "Well, you know, this is important to me as a nonbinary person," and stuff like that, and people be like, "Yay! I support you," and you know, very gender-affirming. But then that doesn't really translate to in-person interactions, so they'll still misgender me.

Jesse's friends are supportive and recognize their nonbinary gender online, but this recognition oftentimes fails to translate into offline interactions. They still have to engage in significant coaching of their friends and reminders to use appropriate terminology. In order to avoid this type of energy investment, Emerson, a white nineteen-year old, only bothers disclosing their gender and pronouns to friends who are already in the so-called queer bubble. Although they by no means try to conceal their nonbinary gender, with a quintessentially queer hairdo (close-cropped on the sides and long and colorful on top), they also do not consider it worthwhile to explain to non-queer friends: "I just kind of tell all my queer friends that understand and know what it is. They use the right pronouns and they are cool with that. Some of my regular friends know, but they don't really … I don't know. Like, they know that it exists, but they still kind of see me as a girl." In an ideal world, Emerson would experience proper gendering from all of their friends, but they anticipate that this social transitioning process would require too much of their energy to be worthwhile. They would have to coach them through the rethinking sex and gender process before they could even begin to redo those relationships.

Conclusion

It is clear that even after nonbinary people disclose their gender, their quest for social recognition requires additional steps that are laborious and sometimes futile. The recipients of their gender disclosures must be willing to change their manner of relating to the nonbinary person in order for that person to effectively "do" their gender within these interactions. Evidently, some loved ones are not willing to make this shift due to their rigid belief systems and others struggle to reprogram their relational habits (though they may have good intentions and improve with time and practice). Furthermore, it is clear that different relationship scripts present different types of interactive obstacles. Parents and siblings must let go of thinking of—and treating—the nonbinary person as a daughter/son and brother/sister, in favor of gender-neutral alternatives. Meanwhile, romantic partners must adjust their sexual scripts in recognition of the nonbinary person's gender—and not all are willing to redo their sexual relationship in this manner.

The relational shift that nonbinary people desire from their loved ones requires a significant amount of labor when compared to other "coming out" case studies. When cisgender people disclose that they are gay or lesbian, they do not necessarily want the recipient of this knowledge to refer to them any differently. In stark contrast, nonbinary people oftentimes disclose their gender in order to achieve some sort of linguistic recognition from others—a goal that requires participation and effort from these other people. The implicit request for labor that is embedded within nonbinary gender disclosures renders this type of "coming out" particularly interactional.

Each time a nonbinary person discloses their gender and explains what nonbinary gender means, the recipient of this knowledge is challenged to rethink the relationship between sex and gender and adjust their habits accordingly. Though these changes occur at a micro-level, it appears that they are having a cumulative effect; as the following chapter will reveal, gender is finally beginning to be "redone" at the institutional level as well. Nonbinary people's "outness" is successfully challenging society to rethink the relationship between sex and gender and thereby redo (expand) gender, though these changes are only just beginning. The next chapter explores these ripple effects in more depth by shifting the analytical focus from interactions within a nonbinary person's intimate inner circle to the opposite extreme: interactions with institutions.

Notes

1. Simon, William, and John H. Gagnon. "Sexual Scripts: Permanence and Change." *Archives of Sexual behavior* 15, no. 2 (1986): 97–120.
2. Testoni, Ines, and Manuela Anna Pinducciu. "Grieving Those Who Still Live: Loss Experienced by Parents of Transgender Children." *Gender Studies* 18, no. 1 (2019): 142–162.
3. For more on biphobic stereotypes, see Eisner's (2013) *Bi: Notes for a Bisexual Revolution.*
4. Beyond gender, Vidal-Ortiz (2002) argues that transgender people are also uniquely situated to demonstrate how people "do sexuality." According to Vidal-Ortiz (2002), transgender people's sexualities "destabilize notions of sexual orientation by opening up the categories themselves to analysis and rigorous scrutiny" (Vidal-Ortiz 2002, 184). As Vidal-Ortiz (2002) notes in his research, some trans men who are attracted to ciswomen consider themselves straight, while others label their sexuality as gay or lesbian. Vidal-Ortiz (2002) proposes that through a symbolic interactionist lens that he calls "doing sexuality," sociologists might come to better appreciate how these sexual orientation labels achieve meaning, become contested, and vary by setting and circumstance. Westbrook (2016) further posits that the study of transgender people's sexualities might even illuminate the process of "redoing"—or restructuring—sexuality beyond binary confines.

Resisting Erasure

"Until the things in the higher up change, I will be prescribed female for most of the main things," Reagan sighed, after explaining all the ways that they try to "do" their nonbinary gender in their daily life. Reagan is relatively successful in rethinking gender, resignifying their gender, and even redoing their relationships beyond the binary framework. However, they still have to contend with binary gender markers on their birth certificates, driver's licenses, and social security cards. They are held accountable to the gender on these forms of official identification when they seek employment, medical care, or register for school. And they find themselves forced into one of the two binary gender boxes on mandatory surveys and forms. Although there is some limited evidence of progressive social change away from this binary-gendered system, which I will discuss at the end of this chapter, nonbinary people still contend with erasure on a routine basis.

There is a term for this type of erasure, called "symbolic annihilation."[1] George Gerbner (1972) first introduced this term to describe how the media's selective erasure of certain groups effectively maintains social inequality. He defined symbolic annihilation as the systematic omission, trivialization, and condemnation of a particular group of people. Six years later, Gaye Tuchman (1978) lent this framework its gendered nuance when she observed that the media continued to systematically omit, trivialize, and condemn women's presence in the workforce despite their exponential rise to power. Such andro-centric media representation perpetuated the illusion of a separate-spheres gender status quo despite the social change that was occurring in the real

H. Darwin, *Redoing Gender*,
https://doi.org/10.1007/978-3-030-83617-7_6

world. In this chapter, I lend symbolic annihilation even further gendered nuance by applying it to the case of nonbinary people within bureaucratic institutions that systematically omit, trivialize, and condemn the existence of gender diversity. This manifestation of symbolic annihilation perpetuates an illusion of a binary gender status quo that simply no longer exists.

Some of the people in my sample—though certainly not all—actively fight back against symbolic annihilation, by insisting upon institutional recognition. This chapter will focus on these people, their experiences, and the contingent process of social change. It cannot be emphasized enough, however, that the majority of my interviewees do *not* fight back, mainly due to concerns about exhaustion management or quite simply out of fear. Hunter explains, "If I were a more outgoing person, by all means I would go to whoever made all the surveys and say 'You need to fix this.' I want to, I just can't do it alone." Confronting the power structure is incredibly daunting and scary, especially when a vital service is at stake, such as medical care or employment.

This chapter illustrates the interactive processes that drive institutional change. In the last five years, society has witnessed the beginning of a shift at the institutional level, as one company after another finally acknowledges gender diversity. But the everyday fear and labor that the most vulnerable parties have had to shoulder while advocating for recognition remains obscured within news coverage of these progressive shifts. It is my hope that this chapter will illuminate the labor that nonbinary people have been performing behind the scenes to compel these institutional changes in the first place—it hasn't happened without a fight.

Creating New Boxes

Surveys and forms routinely require people to specify their gender, even for services that have no real reason to ask for this information, such as a Netflix account. One can simply refuse to designate a gender when prompted to do so on paper forms, but internet forms often require this information to proceed. This is what I call the "binary box dilemma," an impasse that nonbinary people encounter on a regular basis.

To further confound matters, the creators of these surveys and forms oftentimes conflate sex with gender, while asking the individual to clarify whether their *gender* is male or female. Since the majority of my interviewees do identify as biologically male or female, they sometimes graciously assume that the service is more interested in their sex than their gender and select accordingly. However, this dilemma still coerces them into insinuating that they are correspondingly a man or a woman. Thus, it is difficult (and sometimes impossible) for nonbinary people to fight back against symbolic annihilation.

Reagan explains in the following passage why they "pick their battles" when confronted with such erasure:

> If it's medical I put "female" just because it's for medical records. Except actually, I had an MRI on my back a few months ago and I didn't circle either. I just left it blank. And then when I got the copy back the person at the desk circled "female," which really pissed me off. But I just let it go 'cause I don't—I pick my battles and that just didn't feel like one I needed to pick.

Reagan was able to make the decision to avoid misgendering themselves on this medical form only because it was a paper form. And yet, they still found themselves held accountable to the gender binary system by the medical staff in the end, forcefully assigned to the gender that corresponds with their biological sex. They considered confronting the staff about this, but the stakes were simply too high. Their need for medical services outweighed their need for gender recognition by medical staff. Reagan's experience is extremely representative of the sentiments of my other interviewees. Most people feel as though they have no other choice than to let the medical system misgender them if they wish to survive.

Of course, not all services are as indispensable as medical care and sometimes people do assert themselves, as Hunter clarifies: "If it is just like a school survey or something, I actually make a box that says 'other' and check it. But if it is for legal reasons or medical surveys or anything like that, I check 'female' because biologically that is what I am." Addison also occasionally writes in their own box and sometimes takes further corrective measures as well:

> At the last massage I got, I kind of wrote in my own box and wrote "NB." And they even went further and they wanted to know for female clients if you were pregnant or considering it or whatever it says. And I crossed out "female clients" and wrote "clients with uteruses." No one said anything when I turned it in. I feel like I always do these little tiny things and no one says anything.

Again, because this was a paper form, Addison had the liberating option of announcing themselves even though they were not invited to do so. Disappointingly, they didn't receive any engagement from the staff to indicate whether they acknowledged Addison's message or would consider changing their language in the future.

Devin also refuses to play along with nonbinary gender erasure on forms. Of all of the people in this sample, they are by far the most persistent in confronting administrators about this issue:

> I won't fill stuff out if I have to choose a binary gender. And if it's something that I have to do, I'll send a message or an email to whoever created it and say "Hey, my option is not here. What do you want me to do?" And I've had a variety of different types of responses to that. Such as "Just choose whichever one fits best." Or sometimes I get no response, or sometimes I'll get like hostile responses like, "I don't know what you're talking about. Those are the genders."

As with Addison, Devin does not know whether this confrontational labor effects change, but they do it anyway. Devin has clearly decided that this considerable energy expenditure is worthwhile, though most people find it too unsustainable.

Again, most nonbinary people who are hurt by the "binary box dilemma" do not speak up about their pain or fight back against their erasure. Most people are either too conflict-averse, too disillusioned with the prospect of being taken seriously, or simply too scared to say anything. These fears are founded, as illustrated by the experiences of Addison and Devin. When confronted about the harm that this dilemma poses for nonbinary people, institutions are prone to apathy if not abject hostility in response. Nevertheless, people like Devin and Addison persist.

Achieving Recognition at Work and School

It is extremely difficult for nonbinary people to "do" their gender at work or at school unless those who wield power are receptive to acknowledging gender diversity. If a nonbinary person "comes out" at work and their boss and/or coworkers are hostile in response, the only option left to the nonbinary person is to quit. They simply do not have any real power to do anything else at that point.[2] Nevertheless, fourteen of my interviewees have made the decision to be "out" at work. Most of these people work for organizations or bosses that they knew to be LGBTQ-friendly before "coming out." However, this is unfortunately not the case for everyone.

Reagan has encountered resistance from their workplace in almost every way imaginable. Their boss refuses to use Reagan's chosen name (as opposed to their legal name), insisting that he doesn't legally have to oblige. When

Reagan notified him that they would need to go on medical leave following top surgery: "His first reaction was just 'Do what you need to do to be happy.' And then a second thing he said was, 'You're not transitioning, are you?' In like, the most disgusted...like 'Eewwww' face." Understandably, Reagan was shaken by this interaction with their employer, fearing discrimination once they returned to work. And unfortunately, Reagan's workplace troubles were by no means limited to interactions with their hostile boss:

> I had coworkers who would say, like, trying to be funny, "Oh, so which bathroom are you gonna use after your surgery?" Or, "Why don't you save all your money and I can just use a machete and chop off your chest!" And just, like, really inappropriate comments. [...] I did tell my boss and HR about those comments—I didn't say who said them, but I went to them and I said, "Listen, I'm having this surgery and it's already emotionally draining to deal with this identity and this change"—at that time I was dealing with constant rejection from insurance companies, so it was just, like, defeating and deflating and the last thing I needed was trouble at work. And so, I went to them and I was like, "Listen, I'm trying to set myself up for success and I've been hearing all these, like, really inappropriate comments, like, what can we do to support me?" And they were like, "We don't know, we've never dealt with this before, what do you wanna do?" And I was like, "I've never dealt with this before either and that's not my job." So, they kept putting onus back on me and I was just like, "Well, you're HR, you should figure it out." Then nothing ever got done.

Although Reagan's Human Resources Department likely fancied themselves sympathetic, their anemic response to the situation made it crystal clear to Reagan that HR was not to be trusted. I share Reagan's story here because it is illustrative of nonbinary people's worst case scenario if they "come out" in a hostile workplace. From their boss to their coworkers and even down to the Human Resources department, Reagan encountered discrimination, harassment, hostility, and apathy. The only options left to Reagan were quitting or living with these circumstances. There was simply no way for them to change the workplace culture without the cooperation of people in power. Sam shared a similar story about their experiences with harassment and discrimination while working in health care in the South:

> I had a woman that was harassing me at work and threatening to beat me up in the parking lot. And I went to my boss and I was like, "This is not okay and I don't feel safe." And I was working an overnight shift at the time. It was just this woman and three other people. And the boss did not take it seriously at all. She refused to do anything at all to the woman that was harassing me

and so I purposefully found someplace that I felt would be a better place for me at work.

There are plenty of reasons for nonbinary people to conceal their gender in the workplace, as these anecdotes illustrate. Not surprisingly, several interviewees decide to permit or even encourage misgendering at work so as to avoid conflict. As Peyton explains:

> I worked in public schools and in those jobs, I presented as heteronormatively and as gender-normatively as humanly possible for me. Without having my hair…I would like, tie it up and wear it exactly as a man would probably wear long hair…and I kept my voice really low and I tried to be butch as much as I could manage. Because school environments are not particularly great places to be gender non-normative and I also had to work with a lot of students and the kids in these schools were not like, "Hooray for LGBT stuff." They were very not friendly to that sort of thing, I could tell from the get go, so I just kind of let that be…

Avery, a graduate student, feels similar pressure to perform masculinity within their workspace, noting the "power of the suit" to convey their professionalism:

> Being in front of a group of presenters or a group of panelists or whatever, at like a conference and presenting something. Like, "Ok I have to dress in a suit now." Teaching undergrads and wanting to be taken seriously as a teacher…But, I understand the power of the suit. And I understand it is a costume, and that's how I wear it. And I just, I use that power to my advantage.

As a survival mechanism, Peyton and Avery feel compelled to "do masculinity" in the workplace. Only those who work in queer community spaces do not report a similar pressure to present as the gender marker on their legal documentation.

Of course, sometimes people in the workplace go through the motions of inclusivity, but without listening to the needs of their actual nonbinary employees, as Logan explained:

> You definitely have people who are older who just don't get it. Then you have people who I think are more dangerous in a way, who say that they're very into diversity and inclusion. So going back to my old coworker and manager, they're like, "Oh, we know all about diversity and inclusion and this and that"… and they say it, but then they don't.

Logan strongly distrusts seemingly progressive workplaces out of a fear that they are simply trying to profit off of the appearance of inclusivity without implementing policies to bring it into effect. Logan's trepidation is founded; Peyton also discovered the hard way that inclusivity gestures can be superficial at best:

> There was conflict from the very first minute because of the bathrooms in the facility. So, they were like, "Alright, what bathroom do you want to use?" And I was like, "Alright, well, since I'm presenting as a woman, how about the female restroom?" And they said "Okay. The only problem there is that these restrooms are multiuse and so a woman might feel uncomfortable with you using the restroom with them." And I said "Okay." And they're like, "Alright, here's what we'll do. We'll call someone from facilities and they'll install a lock on the door. So that way if you're using the restroom, you can use it alone and lock the door, and we'll treat them as single use restrooms from now on. And if they are comfortable sharing it with you then they can leave the door unlocked." And I said "Okay" and I probably never used the restroom. I just waited until I could go home.

Peyton's HR department was not nearly so apathetic as Reagan's, but they still prioritized cisgender people's comfort and needs over Peyton's. Due to a lack of acceptable options that would leave their sense of dignity intact, Peyton avoided using the restrooms at work altogether. In order to truly redo gender in the workplace, those in power need to listen to their gender-diverse employees and learn more about their desires and needs. Peyton and Logan's employers operate under an assumption that they are already "woke," while doing very little to structurally alter the binary gendering of the workplace itself.

Thankfully, not all workplaces and employers are so resistant to social change. Dakota, a high school teacher in the Bay Area, has begun to coach their coworkers through gender sensitivity and discovered them to be a remarkably receptive audience:

> The presentation was kind of for the benefit of the some of the older folks and there wasn't any big push-back in the question and answer section. Most of the questions were very profitable. [...] I laid out a three-tiered plan. At the bare minimum, if the students express a desire for a specific use of pronouns, then use their goddamn pronouns and if you mess up then just apologize and correct yourself and move on and don't make a big deal about it. The second kind of tier was, if you have heard different pronouns used to describe this kind of student, or if their presentation leads you to express doubt, then ask. Then

the third is ask on your first day, kind of make it public, and make it available to other teacher files if the student comes out and shares this information.

Of course, Dakota's experience in the Bay Area is not representative of experiences in the United States as a whole, but it is still illustrative of how nonbinary people *can* leverage their power in the workplace to institutionally expand gender. Dakota's workplace is doing exactly what Logan suggested, which is listening to gender-diverse employees and learning from their experiences. Dakota provides a rare example of how nonbinary employees can prompt institutions to rethink and redo gender—but only if their employers are receptive to social change. Without such allies in positions of power, nonbinary people can do very little to change the gender structure of the workplace.

Another contingent of interviewees—17, to be exact—were not employees, but rather university students at the time of their interviews. The power imbalance appears to be slightly more manageable for students in the university system than it is for employees in the workplace, but many institutional circumstances remain the same. Teachers possess the power to fail students based on bias, just as employers can fire their employees at whim. Students, like employees, are also at the mercy of the physical structuring of the space, such as the gendering of restrooms, locker rooms, and dormitories. In addition, employees and students both encounter omnipresent "deadnaming"[3] through a default use of their legal names. Universities that default to legal names on class rosters set students up to experience "deadnaming" in class and, without the option of specifying a pronoun on the class roster, students in large classes must simply accept the inevitability of public misgendering on repeat.

However, these interviewees are markedly less afraid of their teachers than my other interviewees were of their employers. Hayden, for example, shared the following anecdote: "Once on a paper in a writing class I addressed myself as 'they' because it was the personal essay and my professor had crossed it out and wrote 'she.' And I talked to him afterwards and he's like 'I'm so sorry. I had no idea. That's fine. You can use it that way.' And I'm like…." Although Hayden walked away from this interaction feeling confident that they would not be misgendered in the future on their writing assignments, they were also perturbed by the professor's insinuation that he possessed the authority to legitimize or delegitimize their pronoun use. Justice also corrects professors when needed:

I'm in a conservation class and one of my professors—it's all identified women—and my professor always starts emails with "Hey ladies, just so you know" or "Hey gals, just so you know" and it doesn't bug me because I know that it's a general blanket term that she's using with everyone but I did respond back with "Hey guys, hey gentlemen" in a joking way and she laughed about it. And now she knows not to use those blanket terms and if she uses blanket terms, to use gender neutral ones. So, the last email I got yesterday I actually got a "Hey y'all" and I was like, thank you for getting it! So even when there are issues with it, my professors aren't assholes about it.

Justice was pleased that their professor seemed relatively amenable to changing her language use to be more gender-inclusive. However, it did require Justice to muster their courage to confront their professor about it, a scenario that is simply too anxiety-provoking for some.

Devin takes the most proactive approach to achieving gender recognition in the university setting, by emailing professors before classes even begin to disclose their gender and pronouns. Devin always hopes that these emails will help them avoid the distress of misgendering in class and save them the awkwardness of correcting a professor in front of classmates. Sometimes this approach is successful, but they also acknowledge that the linguistic shift requires some reminders and coaching on their part. With regard to one professor in particular, Devin says:

She misgenders me sometimes but she acknowledged my email and she said, you know, "Thank you for telling me. If there's anything else that you need from me, let me know." So, after I realized that she was still misgendering me in class I was like, "Hey, is there anything I can do to help you remember my pronouns?" Like, I tried to be helpful like that.

Devin is the most assertive student in my sample by far, but they try to engage with people in an understanding way. They want to expand the range of institutionally recognized genders and know that they will not accomplish this goal if people feel attacked.

Within the university and workplace settings, nonbinary people have to "pick their battles" in the fight for gender recognition. This selection process is often guided by a sense of powerlessness to command respect from one's superiors. Unless the institution or individual in power is receptive to change, nonbinary gender disclosure will simply intensify the eminent danger of discrimination and harassment. Employers and professors must proactively convey that gender diversity is acknowledged and welcome before they can realistically expect their employees and students to disclose their nonbinary gender. People likely do have nonbinary students, employees, classmates, and coworkers, even if they do not know it.

Transnormativity in the Healthcare System

Nonbinary people contend with erasure in the healthcare system as well, largely due to binary constructions of transgender identity that have become institutionalized. Many of my interviewees have stumbled upon this particular manifestation of the gender binary—or in this case, what I call the "transgender binary"—while pursuing treatment for mental or physical health needs related to gender.

Twenty-nine of my nonbinary interviewees experience some form of body dysphoria (whether or not they have received an official diagnosis, and whether or not they identify with the transgender label). Among these 29 people, 15 have made changes to their body through the aid of hormone therapy or surgery. Thirteen others were considering pursuing such changes at the time of this interview. Problematically, health insurance policies tend to require specific diagnoses before people can access hormone replacement therapy and gender confirmation surgeries—diagnoses which revolve around the notion that all trans individuals desire a binary gender transition.[4] Some countries, like Denmark, even require that the individual commits to a binary gender transition in order to access much-needed procedures like HRT or top surgery. However, not all nonbinary people want the effects of hormone therapy even if they do pursue top surgery (and vice versa).

Unfortunately, this approach to medical transitioning is oftentimes invalidated by insurance companies and nonbinary people possess very little power to push back against this transgender binary within the healthcare system. Lane, a white 24-year-old Danish interviewee, initially pursued the state-sponsored medical transition option before it became too upsetting:

> For me personally, I reached the stage where I just couldn't wait anymore. Like, this whole process of waiting and not knowing if I could… if I would be approved for hormone and so on, like it was … I am still healing from that whole thing. It was so difficult for me, mental health wise. There's a lot of waiting time just to get to, you know, go to these appointments. It's… the appointments themselves has been going on for about a year before I got approved.

Jes further explained that this incentivized "package deal" would not help them achieve their gender even if it was affordable: "I don't want testosterone, I don't want a beard. I don't want, like… the look of boys or anything. I just want the breasts removed. So, I think it would be safer and easier for me to just save up the money to go to Germany." Like Jes, Lane eventually quit their government-subsidized program and opted to pay out of pocket for their hormones at a private clinic in Germany that is known for being LGBTQ-friendly. Through this decision, Jes and Lane took back their power from a system that was trying to shape their gender identity and prospective body into conformity with the binary transgender narrative. However, this is a privileged decision that is only available to those who have money.

Reagan, who lives in the United States, encountered similar restrictions to those that my Danish respondents recounted within the government-regulated transition process—their insurance would only cover top surgery if they were also on hormones. Their surgery was denied three times due to their refusal to undergo hormone replacement therapy that they did not need or desire. Unlike Lane and Jes, Reagan did fight back against the erasure of transgender diversity within the healthcare system. They hired a lawyer to help them negotiate with the insurance company and circumnavigate these institutional accountability structures:

> I told her everything and sent her the letters from all my therapists and my medical doctor, saying this was medically necessary for my health. And she fought for me. She spoke to legal department of Empire Blue Cross Blue Shield and got them to overturn their denial. She said she was pretty sure that they were gonna then change their policy, 'cause I think if they do it for me they have to do it for other people, is what I understood. Which I feel really great about 'cause if my fighting it—or really her fighting it—makes it easier for other people, then I feel really happy about that. They ended up covering the whole thing, which was amazing.

As with my Danish interviewees, Reagan was given two options: begin hormones in order to gain access to top surgery or live with dysphoria due to their breast tissue. Instead of choosing one of these equally unacceptable options, Reagan fought the system and ultimately succeeded in forcing it to acknowledge the need for a third option. By refusing to be held accountable to the medical model of transgender and its binary gendered logic, Reagan successfully catalyzed the "redoing" of gender at the institutionalized level.

Four other interviewees clarified that they have been fortunate enough to easily access their desired and needed services. For example, Alex was surprised by how quickly they acquired approval for hormone therapy:

> In mid-October I went to the session and she was like, "How are you doing today?" And I was like, "I want to be on hormones before the end of October." And she was like, "All right! I've been waiting for that. I have the letter all written out. Now we just need to plug in the relevant information. What doctor do you want to go to?" And we found a doctor and the second week of November I went to him and had a 10-minute meeting with him and he just

went, "Looks good to me, here's your prescription." And had my pills by the end of the day.

This experience diverges sharply from the arduous process that my Danish respondents described, as well as the experience of some Americans with other insurance plans. Jack also had a positive experience with the medical system when they requested hormones and top surgery. Their progressive medical institution happily maneuvered around insurance caveats in order to accommodate Jack's needs: "Basically, I've rolled up to the clinic and been like, 'Hey, I want to get started, what do I need?' And they're like, 'Oh, here, we have a form letter for you because that's what the insurance will ask for.'".

These exceptions are certainly refreshing to hear, but they still prove the rule of nonbinary erasure. Insurance policies and healthcare bureaucracy still have a long way to go toward acknowledging gender—and transgender—diversity. Those who fit neatly within the transnormative narrative of being "born in the wrong body" are deemed legitimately in need of gender confirmation procedures,[5] while nonbinary people's needs are somehow less legitimate. Few of my interviewees have been able to push back against this transgender binary.

Conclusion

Nonbinary people continue to experience symbolic annihilation at the institutional level within our society. This erasure is perpetuated by the stubborn conflation of sex and gender that persists on formal surveys, forms, and identification documents. Furthermore, this erasure has far-flung implications for nonbinary people, as they are held accountable to these formal designations by institutions such as the healthcare system, the legal system, the workplace, and universities. Thus, erasure is not only a mere act of symbolic violence, but also a barricade to nonbinary people's ability to "do" and embody their gender. In short, symbolic annihilation functions as the most intransigent safeguard against social change. Due to nonbinary people's powerlessness within these institutional interactions, they have little recourse but to accept their gender's erasure. Some people have persisted in fighting for gender recognition, identified allies in positions of power, and succeeded in catalyzing institutional shifts. However, these anecdotes are few and far between.

Notes

1. George Gerbner (1972) and Gaye Tuchman (1978).
2. Title VII offers some measure of protection against sex discrimination in the workplace, but employers are still entitled to coerce their employees to conform to their "normative" guidelines—even if this requires employees to compromise an aspect of self-expression that is central to their identity (Clements 2009).
3. "Deadnaming" is a colloquial way to refer to the practice of ignoring a trans individual's chosen name and calling them by their birth name instead.
4. Johnson (2016).
5. Gender confirmation procedures are also frequently time-consuming and costly for trans men and trans women.

Regression and Progress

I made an effort to keep in touch with my interviewees throughout the years, as I analyzed and eventually published this data. I had promised to do so, since I could not offer them a monetary stipend for their time; at the very least, I wanted them to have access to the fruits of our collective labor and to correct me if I ever misunderstood their words. Unfortunately, as the years passed, more and more emails began to bounce back to me as people graduated from universities and lost access to their institutional email addresses or simply changed email addresses that had previously contained "deadnames." Nevertheless, I continued to send out article manuscripts as I prepared to submit them to journals, alongside updates on my project's progress.

One day, Harley replied to one of these email blasts to tell me how bizarre it felt to read excerpts from our interview. Even though everything they said had been true at the time, their experience of their gender had changed dramatically in the four years since then. "I bet my answers would be totally different if you asked me the same questions today," they concluded. I wasn't able to shake this conversation as I plowed onward with my text analysis and publication process, wondering how many other participants would also like the chance to answer my questions again, four years later.

When I realized that these four years mapped almost perfectly onto the presidency of Donald Trump, I decided to proceed with follow-up interviews.[1] The Trump era introduced a number of restrictive and discriminatory policies against transgender and nonbinary people, which are detailed on the Trump Accountability Project website, run by the Gay and Lesbian Alliance

© The Author(s), under exclusive license to Springer Nature
Switzerland AG 2022
H. Darwin, *Redoing Gender*,
https://doi.org/10.1007/978-3-030-83617-7_7

Against Defamation.[2] His administration erased all mentions of LGBTQ people from all websites connected to the White House, Department of State, and Department of Labor, as well as from the census and numerous other government surveys. He appointed a plethora of anti-LGBTQ officials, including but not limited to his Vice President, Mike Pence. He banned transgender service members from serving "in any capacity" in the US military. His Justice Department allowed for "religious exemptions" regarding protections against discrimination for LGBTQ people. Staff at the Centers for Disease Control and Prevention were instructed not to use the word "transgender" in official budget documents. The Department of Education formally declined to investigate discrimination claims by transgender students regarding restroom use. Housing and Urban Development announced a new rule allowing single-sex homeless shelters to turn away transgender people. The Trump Administration rolled back protections for incarcerated transgender people and even attempted to revoke Title IX protections against workplace discrimination for transgender people, arguing that it does not constitute sex discrimination. I cannot emphasize enough that this list is far from complete.

While it is tempting to think of social progress as a linear trajectory, there were plenty of reasons to suspect that nonbinary people's lives might have actually become more difficult over the last four years. I didn't know what to expect, but I wanted to give my participants a chance to tell me whether it had become easier or harder to be nonbinary in society since our last interview. And I also simply wanted to check in with their gender journeys.

* * *

Harley was right—their answers to my questions were dramatically different this time around, as they were for most people who had only just realized they were nonbinary slightly before our initial interview. When I first spoke to Harley, they were still using their birth name, hadn't told many people about their gender, and felt uncomfortable using the transgender label. Four years later, they had started to proudly use the transgender label, had changed their name to Harley, stopped wearing dresses and other overtly feminine-coded clothing, and even changed the way they moved their body to incorporate fewer feminine-coded gestures:

> I have changed the way I walk. So, it mirrors how men walk more. And I've been doing more training with dance movement to be more masculine, I guess, to move in a more masculine way. It's been a challenge. Because, you know, learning from a very small age, like, this is the way I move. This is the way

I like to dance. This is the way I'm supposed to be moving with this body. And, yeah, coming up against that realizing, oh, wow, okay. There are huge differences in the ways that men and women move. And I want to choose at least. So, training myself out of those defaults has been a challenge for sure.

As a dance instructor and performer, Harley has become increasingly attuned to the gendering of movement. They call upon this expertise as they move forward with their gender transition and literally take it into their body.

When I asked Harley whether it's gotten any easier to be a nonbinary person in society over the last four years, they replied quickly in the affirmative:

I think that there are more examples of nonbinary folks. Sam Smith came out as a nonbinary gentleman. And *Merriam Webster's* word of the year was singular they. There definitely are more examples. There are more nonbinary characters and media. And that's been amazing, to have any representation or any amount of familiarity. And especially in the Bay Area, there are quite a few nonbinary folks. One of my partners' housemates came out as nonbinary recently. I think it is easier just because there's more of us that are more visible. We've kind of gotten to that annoying place where like, people who don't know much will be like, "Oh, they're just identifying as nonbinary because it's popular, because they want to be special." So that's pretty annoying. But, generally speaking, I think it is a little bit easier than it was before.

Harley attributes the Bay Area public's increasing familiarity with gender diversity to media representation, though they also acknowledge the downside of this sudden flurry of visibility: that cisgender people mistakenly assume people are disingenuously following a trend. And indeed, readers might recall that Harley themselves voiced concerns about being dismissed as a "transtrender" in our original interview, before they started using they/them pronouns or identifying with the transgender label.

In many ways, Harley's interview provides a useful starting off point for this chapter, which primarily asks whether society's recognition of gender diversity continues to expand as time marches on. This is an important question to ask while analyzing any sort of social change. It was tempting for some of my interviewees to jump at the opportunity to say that yes, it has gotten so much easier four years later. However, these initially enthusiastic responses were often followed by caveats and qualifications, especially when I gently pointed out that these four years mapped onto the Trump era.[3]

Did institutional shifts continue in a progressive trajectory during these four years? What about relational shifts? Threats from strangers? Did my interviewees continue to "rethink" sex and gender as they settled further into their nonbinary gender? In short, has the "redoing of gender" continued unabated? Or not so much? These were my primary curiosities as I checked back in.

Social Progress Narratives

Like Harley, Parker is extremely optimistic about the changes they have witnessed in society over the last four years. The reader might remember Parker as the Filipino graduate student with long nails who plucked their body hair. By the time of this interview, Parker was living in Florida with their long-term partner in an area with a vibrant LGBTQ community. According to Parker, "We're just heading toward a place where we understand that the world is complex, and that people are complex, and that that's okay. Right. And that not everybody has to subscribe to the things that they've been socialized to believe is how they should act." Parker doesn't wear their fingernails long anymore out of practical rock-climbing considerations, but they have started to shave their full body and identify more firmly as queer. They still don't bother trying to explain their gender to their parents or to older people in general, but they feel like Millennials and Gen Z understand things like their pronouns without requiring much explanation.

Hayden agrees with Parker that there seems to be a generational difference that points to a more expansive gender future. Hayden was a twenty-one-year-old undergraduate student when we first spoke. Even then, they made a point to include their pronouns in their email signature line and were "out" to their family—including their hostile brother who works as a pastor. In the last four years, they have settled into their nonbinary gender even more openly. They buzzed off their hair, started binding their chest, and entered their first long-term romantic relationship as a nonbinary person. They feel fairly confident that they will pursue top surgery in the future. Hayden expressed pride in how far they've come in four years' time, attributing their newfound confidence at least in part to proliferating media representation:

> I think I've seen more representation in the past couple of years, both through people's advocacy and media and all these different things. And obviously, the internet is blowing up right now with folks of all different identities. And I think that's great. In my own life, it's gotten easier just in the sense that I'm more confident and less ashamed of who I am. So, I'm definitely able to, you know, confront things when I see them.

When I pointedly asked whether the Trump era has made life more difficult for them, Hayden surprised me by saying:

> You know, it's actually made—for me—made things better. I'm so much more likely to advocate for things that I believe in, like, in the moment it's happening, because him becoming president has shown me how many people there are in this country who really feel like he's on the right path and doing good things. And has the right ideals. And I'm like, "That's not true."

Hayden has a relatively timid disposition in general, permeating their interview responses with nervous laughter. Yet, despite their conciliatory demeanor, they felt called to situate themselves on the frontlines of the gender revolution during the Trump era. The stakes simply became too high for them to shy away from confrontation.

Meanwhile, Morgan doesn't bother getting into fights with people about their gender anymore. Like Hayden, Morgan had been twenty-one and very recently "out" when we last spoke, though they already firmly identified with the transgender label and used they/them pronouns. The biggest change for them since our last interview revolves around their sexual orientation group membership, as they have since shifted from using "queer" to "lesbian." Morgan used to feel pressure to distance themselves from all things feminine-encoded in order to be nonbinary, but as they've become more comfortable and confident, they've begun to reclaim some of these things. They no longer care if they make sense to anyone else: "It has become less about explaining what it means and more about explaining that you need to respect me no matter what you believe." Morgan does not exist to serve cisgender people. Their goal is to achieve basic social recognition and respect, whether people fully understand their gender or not.

Rhiannon also doesn't think that cisgender people understand what it means to be nonbinary yet. Rhiannon was 24 when we last spoke, using the "graygender" label, and hesitant to involve themselves in the LGBTQ community or to announce their pronouns as "they/them." Rhiannon is unconvinced that the redoing of gender has spread throughout society on a deep ideological level. And yet, at the same time, people have pleasantly surprised them since they started coming out: "I do feel like the people around me are more primed to understand and help than I had originally assumed that they would be. And I don't know if that's because I wasn't coming out as much four years ago or because things have changed." However, Rhiannon is skeptical about what this shift actually implies about people's embrace of gender diversity:

I want to say I think certain pockets of society are more familiar with it. I definitely think it's a concept that's out there more now. I don't know, I can't say that, like, people are more *accepting* of it. But I think I could say that people are more familiar with it as more and more people become visible. More and more people become visible and more and more people become out and people with platforms are coming out now. And so, I think it's reaching more people, but I can't say with certainty that people are—even if it reaches them—that they're internalizing it, or if they're saying like, "Oh, that's a thing." And like, "Maybe I know someone nonbinary." Or if they're just saying, like, "Well, that's some fucking thing the queer community is doing these days." Like, "I'm not really internalizing or, like, acknowledging it on a more personal level."

To Rhiannon, it appears that cisgender people simply "pride themselves on not making a fuss" about pronouns, but still inwardly roll their eyes about it.

People pride themselves on not making a fuss about gender diversity in part because of the media's embrace of it as a cool and edgy phenomenon. Even if it's only on a superficial level, the exponential media embrace of gender-diverse characters and plotlines seems to have helped spread awareness of gender diversity on a large scale among cisgender people. As Morgan said:

It's so much easier. With all the, like, media, television, music, I feel like everyone's just coming out left and right. And with all the Gen Z's, I love them, like, they're amazing. They're really doing something that like, you know, Millennials couldn't really do. They're just putting it out there, going for it and not explaining themselves to anyone. I love that. I feel like it's just been so much easier for kids to come out and be supported. And that's something that like, I'm so glad is there.

Increased media representation and awareness results in less explanatory labor for nonbinary people when they "come out." When they say "I'm nonbinary," they don't have to brace themselves for the previously ubiquitous response of "What's that?" This cultural shift has made it easier for nonbinary people to achieve social recognition as nonbinary.

"Pendulum Swing" Narratives

However, not everyone's so sure that society has become an easier place to be nonbinary. Kazi is one such person. Kazi was in law school at the time of our follow-up interview, in a serious committed relationship, and identifying as a nonbinary trans man. As with Rhiannon, Kazi video conferenced me from their childhood home where they were staying temporarily due to coronavirus—and as with Rhiannon, this setting is not a particularly welcoming space for their gender or their sexuality. Their parents have struggled to accept them over the years and continue to send out their "marriage CV" to parents of marriageable sons within their Bengali Muslim community. Kazi reported all of this to me with a smirk and an eyeroll, indicating that it doesn't bother them too much since they are not even single.

When I last spoke with Kazi, they were serving in a leadership capacity within their university's Transgender Alliance and thus engaging in considerable explanatory labor on behalf of the transgender community. They report that they are still providing this labor four years later, though it has assumed a more nuanced form due to increased media representation of nonbinary celebrities:

> I think I'm explaining still, but I think the basic explaining was being like, well, there's no man or woman. I think normal people understand that. But I think now it's like, we've skipped the basics. And now I'm fully in defense mode or fully in correction mode. I've had friends who are very nice be like, "I don't understand what's going on. It's like Sam Smith, right?" And I'm like, "Well, here we go."

Kazi does not want their experience of their gender to be conflated with Sam Smith's, but since this hyper-visible celebrity "came out," that has become the reference point for many people. Kazi is grateful that people are at least minimally aware of the notion of gender diversity, but they also worry that such exposure leads the public to overly simplify nonbinary gender. In Kazi's words, "The media has created this sort of false sense of relief. Not everyone in the media has been good for us." Increased public discourse about nonbinary gender opens the floodgates to misunderstandings, dismissal, and the proliferation of more sophisticated forms of discrimination: "It's going so fast that I'm always worried about the blowback."

Cleo also observes a sort of pendulum swing between progressive and regressive outcomes of nonbinary visibility, describing social change as a "seesaw." Cleo was 23 and unemployed when we last spoke, living with her grandmother in an ultra-Orthodox Jewish neighborhood where she felt hyper-visible as queer. Her circumstances had not changed four years later, but the same could not be said for her body. Cleo's face was noticeably rounder from hormone therapy and her dark hair was much longer, down to her jawline and middle-parted. When we last spoke, Cleo used "they/them" pronouns and identified as genderfluid. At the time of this follow-up interview, she used "she/her" pronouns and identified as a nonbinary transfemme.

Cleo video conferenced me from her room in her grandmother's house where she feels increasingly unsafe and unhappy. We spoke while she curled up in bed with her blanket pulled up to her chin. Like Kazi, Cleo acknowledges that some good might have come out of increased media representation, but she still encounters so much resistance, discrimination, and threats of violence that it's difficult for her to say that anything has gotten "better." In her words:

> There's an empowering part of my experience of being more open. And there's a fearful part. And something that's really deteriorated me mentally is that the more I've experienced backlash from the world for simply existing, for simply presenting myself, for simply wanting to exist for myself, and wanting to just simply remind the world "I want to be respected, I want to be free, I want to be accepted, I want to be loved, I want to be affirmed." I don't want to be ostracized. I'm getting physical, mental…all these messages from this world in violent ways, that I'm not allowed to exist. And if I do exist, I will be harmed, and I will be pushed back. And I won't be believed.

Cleo experiences the shift in media representation as a hollow invitation to become more "out" and open about her gender while the surrounding culture remains unchanged. The more visible she and other gender-diverse people become, the more loudly and violently the opposition reacts.

Mason is also a little nervous about potential backlash against the mainstream culture's embrace of transgender: "I think it's hard to say that more visibility is necessarily a *good* thing. I think it can be beneficial in terms of like, raising awareness about trans issues and about nonbinary experiences. But I do think the big increase in violence is probably linked to that too." This omnipresent threat of violence does not deter Mason from embracing and expressing their gender, but it is never far from their mind. When we last spoke, Mason worked in a university setting where they were too afraid to experiment with their gender expression. Four years later, Mason had a much more feminine-encoded appearance, with shoulder-length silky black hair, jewel-toned makeup, and jewelry. Mason began HRT shortly after we first spoke, which has had a noticeably softening effect on their face. They feel more comfortable identifying with the transgender label now that they are pursuing a medical transitioning process. However, they made a point to clarify that they do not identify as a woman—they are still firmly nonbinary. They have had a surprisingly successful time explaining this to people: "I never feel like people don't know nonbinary, other than maybe not fully understanding what it means."

According to these rather ambivalent interviewees, social progress isn't so much a linear trajectory; rather, it operates like a seesaw or a pendulum swing. After swinging dramatically in one direction, it swings the opposite direction with nearly equal force, creating a back-and-forth motion that only gradually settles into stasis. Sure, people are more familiar with the notion of gender diversity as time marches on. However, they are also more prone to essentialize it, reduce it to celebrity cover stories, and ultimately dismiss it as a fad. As Mason said, increased visibility is not always a good thing.

Regression Narratives

And finally, some of my interviewees feel that in several ways society has become a more *difficult* place for nonbinary people to be out and proud four years later. However, whether this hostility results from increased media visibility, Trump era politics or the coronavirus crisis remains up for debate.

Jaylen shared this pessimistic assessment with me while out on a walk with their two nonbinary partners in Florida. When we last spoke, Jaylen was 25 and identified as a genderqueer butch lesbian woman. At the time of this follow-up interview, they identified as trans and used they/them pronouns as well as she/her pronouns. However, labels weren't foremost on their mind during our conversation. Instead, they wanted to share how their disability and healing journey have affected their experience of their gender. Apparently when we last spoke, Jaylen could barely walk. I was surprised that they didn't mention this at all at the time. They were injured during their time in the Peace Corp and needed a series of back surgeries that each required lengthy recovery periods. Since they are a masculine "top" in bed, this was a very compromising time period for their gendered sense of self. Jaylen has been enjoying the ability to walk again, but also to have sex the way they experience as gender-affirming. They have also begun to engage in other rugged and gender-affirming activities, like working in construction.

When I asked them if they felt like it has become more or less difficult being nonbinary in society, they shared that the Trump era has made them fear violence in a way that they haven't for a while:

> I think people are feeling emboldened. I think people are getting smarter about how they attack trans people, you know, I think they're learning more intimately what the community is like, so they're figuring out, you know, places they can kind of go after us. Now, the Trump era definitely freaks me out. Because, you know, I live in the rural south. So, people are still staring out the window, their cars, stuff like that, you know. I feel different when I'm, like,

on the West Coast or Portland or something like that. But in rural Florida, it's still pretty intense.

Jaylen is not as lucky as most of my interviewees, who live their lives in sheltered queer bubbles. Rather, Jaylen lives face to face with people who still misunderstand and fear their presence in the world. Under the Trump era, this constant surveillance has begun to feel increasingly threatening.

Avery also remains unconvinced that society has become more welcoming to gender diversity during the Trump era, though this is mainly due to the timing of the coronavirus pandemic. When we last spoke, Avery was a 28-year-old graduate student who identified as nonbinary, but not as transgender. The last four years have been incredibly hard for Avery. They dropped out of graduate school following a breakup from their fiancé, a descent into hard drugs, and suicidal ideation. After they moved back to their hometown to live with their parents, they continued to struggle with drug addiction, leading to multiple arrests. By the time we spoke, they were committed to turning their life around. They had been clean and sober for some time and wanted to make sure that it stayed that way during the coronavirus lockdown. They continued their Narcotics Anonymous meetings in quarantine via Skype and avoided friends who reminded them of that time in their life.

Avery did not identify as nonbinary at the time of this follow-up interview, but they also didn't feel entirely comfortable calling themselves a man. Nevertheless, out of respect for their parents who they were still living with, they made a point to present in a gender-normative way, conforming to the expectations of their surrounding community. Their primary objective was to simply get along and not make waves. When I asked Avery if it has become any easier to be nonbinary in society, they answered rather confidently in the negative:

> I think that people have become more accepting of trans people. But for nonbinary, they're still very hesitant to accept it because they don't understand. And especially in times right now, when we're about in an election cycle. That's the last thing they get. That's the last thing the public wants to talk about. The last thing they want to hear about. You know, I think it's important, but it always gets put on the back burner in times of crisis like these. But it's always like that with identity politics. You get made to feel stupid or not important for trying to talk about it when they're like, "People are dying!" Yeah, that's important. But, you know, human lives are important too. Considering the amount of mental health issues that people face, the amount of suicide rates of queer teens, dropout rates, homelessness rates of trans people, especially trans women, HIV rates, all that…there's a lot to it. There's a lot of human lives

still at risk because of, you know, either oppression or people not being able to come out. Or people facing harsh consequences for coming out.

Kazi echoed Avery's sentiment that "identity politics" are low on society's list of priorities: "What's our priority right now? Like, right, are we fighting for it? Can we say this is the time that we fight for our gender rights, when we're just fighting for the right to survive in this world?".

Between the chaos of the Trump era and the existential crisis posed by coronavirus, Kazi, Avery, and others feel like the gender revolution has stalled, put on indefinite hold for a later day. But as Avery cynically observes, it always seems to get "put on the back burner," compared to the myriad other social issues that plague society at any point in time. So, when is the right time to focus on redoing gender as a society? The longer we wait, the more people suffer and even die, as Avery emphasized.

Indeed, the lingering threat of violence was not far from my interviewees' minds when they weighed in on the state of affairs in 2020. Most people included at least a token acknowledgment of the spate of murders of black trans women, while some even recounted anecdotes about fearing for their own safety in recent times. As Cleo shared:

> Last week, I was walking home and feeding someone who was homeless, and a group of girls with their boyfriends harassed me and trashed a 711 store and threw items at me, and then recorded me to mock me, as they were trying to beat up a trans person to show their friends their dominance. And I was able to do the best I could to deescalate and avoid that situation. But I was traumatized. And it made me just internalize that still today the world often perceives me as an alien, as a freak, as a mockery. As someone who is confused and illegitimate.

Cleo's mental health continues to suffer as they contend with casual street harassment from strangers in New York City. Despite evidence of progressive relational shifts and institutional shifts, strangers still pose a very real and pressing threat to nonbinary people, especially trans femme people of color such as Cleo. Discrimination, prejudice, and violence remain key regulatory devices of the self-appointed gender-police. These interactions remind nonbinary people of the looming dangers of recognition in a hostile world.

Managing Difference

A simple identity disclosure is insufficient when others do not know what that identity means and possibly disagree that it can even exist. Thus, the demands of the "coming out career" for nonbinary people extend far beyond a simple declarative statement, as this book has made quite clear. Nonbinary people must also educate the public, coach them through how to act, remind them when they mess up, and deal with potentially volatile emotional reactions from cisgender people in the process. Throughout all of this, they must carefully manage their emotions and exhaustion levels lest they burn out.

Burning out is a very real risk to nonbinary people and to the continuing expansion of gender in society. Four years later, fewer of my interviewees fight for recognition with the same passion and regularity as they did before. They are tired and worried about their mental and emotional well-being. As Parker explains, "Nobody wants to go through this show, like, the song and dance of explaining gender identity and performativity to every person they meet." Avery voices a similar sentiment:

> I've gone through so much in my life now that the last thing I want to do is to get into an argument with somebody about sexuality and gender, if it's not going to be respectful. You know what I'm saying? Yeah, it can be an argument or a debate, but it's got to be respectful. And if they start to get mad, I mean, I walk away.

Due to the predictability of this type of resistance, some people have unsurprisingly given up on general society. As Lane explains, "I don't care that much anymore. People can pretty much use any pronouns for me even though all of this stuff feels weird. But I don't want to spend my energy worrying about it. Because the people that matter, they use the right pronouns for me." Lane is part of a contingent that has essentially retreated from mainstream society, relegating their social interactions to queer culture where understandings about gender diversity are more advanced. Through this approach, nonbinary people can conserve their energy.

Morgan emphatically declares that nonbinary people are tired of waiting for the public to "understand" their gender—as though this type of epiphany is necessary in order to act respectfully. Morgan related this to their sudden realization that other people will never truly understand what it means for them to live with chronic pain. Similarly, cisgender people will never understand what it's like to live with constant gender discomfort. But just because other people don't personally feel those sensations does not mean that they can dismiss other people's experiences of them. Since they had this realization,

Morgan is less willing to expend explanatory labor. Instead, they express frustration that cisgender people don't invest effort into learning about nonbinary gender on their own:

> I'm sick of educating everyone around me. There's Google, you can go use it, you can find it. Like, I can only explain so much what it means. Because it's not really…people don't really care what it means. They just want to understand something they're not going to understand. They want to have an experience they're not going to experience and I can't explain that away.

Morgan doesn't even bother trying to explain their gender to people who they think will be too confused and perhaps willfully so: "I can only do so much. So, I do what I can. And I educate them when I can. But if it just turns like to mush every single time, it's not worth my effort."

That isn't to say that everyone has given up on educating the public and fighting for recognition. But the longer people fight, the more fatigued they become, and the more boundaries they need to erect in order to protect themselves. No one explained this careful consideration of identity management and exhaustion management better than Rhiannon:

> I'm used to being the one to take on education capacities. And sometimes it's to protect other nonbinary people. Like, "Okay, if I educate this person now, then maybe it'll save another person having to educate them in the future." But I think recently, and it was really just within the last year, I've come to understand the power of saying to someone, like, "I don't have the emotional capacity to have this conversation right now. I can, you know, text you or email you resources if you want to get some of your questions answered."

Rhiannon used to be much more engaged on the frontlines of the "gender revolution," providing free educational labor rather indiscriminately whenever misgendering occurred. However, when that approach began to produce early warning signs of "burnout," they knew that they would have to come up with a more sustainable long-term strategy. They still try to be friendly and encouraging while redirecting people to the necessary resources, but they don't take it all on themselves anymore.

Exhaustion is a key guiding consideration in whether and under what circumstances nonbinary people "come out." However, safety considerations rank as a close second, especially for the people of color in my sample, as Cleo demonstrated in the previous section. Even Reagan, who is white, frequently alluded to safety concerns while explaining their thought process behind correcting people:

The other piece of it is safety. Like, is it safe? Am I in a safe place? To correct someone? Like, if I'm in an Uber, right? Not gonna correct the driver. You know, depending on what state I'm in, I might not even correct the waitress or waiter or the server. You know, so that also plays into that equation.

Unfortunately, safety is not actually so easy to predict. Even within presumably progressive spaces and places, nonbinary people are never entirely safe from the omnipresent threat of violence, which Cleo is quick to point out: "It's a burden to be the minority in a world that is stacked against you. Like, I'm in New York City and I have the law on my side. But it doesn't mean culturally and socially, I feel safe. And I do feel that I need to hide and conform in many ways to feel safe." The possibility of an attack is never far from Cleo's mind. Physical well-being is as pressing of a consideration as emotional well-being among my interviewees.

Conclusion

It would seem that the pendulum swing model is the most accurate assessment of how the "redoing of gender" is going four years later. Nonbinary people have made tentative gains within society, but these gains are fragile and unevenly distributed. People's experiences of these gains vary dramatically depending on their cultural field and social network. This pendulum swings the most noticeably at the institutional level, which we saw when President Biden immediately set to work undoing Donald Trump's discriminatory policies against trans and nonbinary Americans. There is no reason to doubt that another reactionary swing against gender diversity looms in the near future, but politics cannot undo the rethinking and redoing of gender that has taken place at the individual and interactional levels in the meantime. Policy reversals can only do so much to deny people's lived realities, especially once gender diversity has been recognized and embraced by the wider culture, as evidenced through media representation. The secret of gender diversity has come out of the closet and there's no going back. The "Gender Revolution" is here—but it isn't happening without an active daily fight at the interpersonal level against self-appointed members of the gender-police.

Notes

1. I envisioned this follow-up process as a feminist methodological experiment. I wanted to give my participants the opportunity to compare and contrast their gendered experiences and identity four years ago to today, but without their previous answers influencing their new answers. Thus, after each follow-up interview, in which I asked the same general questions as before (omitting original questions that failed to produce interesting findings or conversation the last time around), I sent my participants the transcript of our original interview. People voiced considerable enthusiasm over the prospect of gaining access to their transcript and revisiting their past self. I asked them to read it before too much time could pass, hopefully within a week of our follow-up interview, and let me know how they would analyze the data. How do they think their gender has changed or stayed the same? Has it gotten any easier to be nonbinary in society as time moves on? I framed this invitation with an acknowledgement that they are the experts of their gender, not me; in the end, all I know is what they happened to tell me in the course of our interviews. They seemed to appreciate that I extended them an opportunity to weigh in on the analytical process, but in the end only half of them sent me written reflections (despite my reminders). Most of these responses were quite short and didn't really offer new material beyond what they said in the follow-up interview. Therefore, I base this chapter primarily upon the transcripts of the follow-up interviews themselves.
2. "The Trump Accountability Project," *Gay & Lesbian Alliance Against Defamation.* Accessed January 31, 2021. https://www.glaad.org/tap/donald-trump.
3. Most people acknowledged this timing overlap themselves during the course of our interview—I only brought it up if they didn't organically mention anything about it by the end.

Conclusion

This book walked you through the various forms of labor that nonbinary people—primarily in and from the United States—perform while trying to interactively "do" their gender. To recap, the famous "doing gender" model posits that people are not inherently born with a gender, but rather learn how to "do" gender. They internalize these lessons after prolonged exposure to them in society. Other people hold them accountable to gender ideals and norms in their everyday life from birth-onward, as do institutions.

I began this book by showing you how these messages mess with people's heads when they start to feel like their gender might not fit in the binary "man" and "woman" categories. Unable to make sense of their gender discomfort (dysphoria) within the gender binary system, they either go into denial, assume they must simply be experiencing gender dysphoria due to their sexuality, or otherwise assume they must be a trans man/trans woman. Before they can even realize that their gender *is* nonbinary, they must rethink sex and gender to allow for a nonbinary gender category's existence in the first place. Sometimes—though not always—this rethinking process also requires them to rethink their sexual orientation. Some people automatically identify as transgender once they realize they are neither a man nor a woman, but this is not the case across the board. Plenty of nonbinary people maintain ambivalence about claiming the transgender label because they do not feel like they are "transgender enough," or because they feel that there is an important difference between the transgender experience and their own.

© The Author(s), under exclusive license to Springer Nature
Switzerland AG 2022
H. Darwin, *Redoing Gender*,
https://doi.org/10.1007/978-3-030-83617-7_8

Gender nonbinary people are a diverse group in their own right and not a straightforward subcategory of transgender.

After realizing that they are nonbinary, people must decide whether and how to convey this information to others. I detailed various visual cues that my interviewees employ to thwart easy categorization as "man" or "woman," as well as their multifarious pronoun specification practices. A common theme throughout the pronoun discussion revolved around exhaustion and emotion management. If the interaction is a one-time thing or the person does not seem particularly open-minded, my interviewees tend to permit misgendering. It is simply too exhausting and dangerous to indiscriminately "come out" to everyone. This isn't an active attempt to "pass" as cisgender, so much as a strategy that protects nonbinary people from burnout during their coming out careers.

While nonbinary people often permit misgendering from strangers, acquaintances, colleagues, and employers, it is generally considered worthwhile to "come out" to family members, close friends, and romantic partners. This interactive process can be tricky, however, because "coming out" is not just a simple disclosure, as we have discussed. Nonbinary people must also oftentimes prepare themselves to educate the other person about gender, coach them through their desired "relational shift," remind them when they mess up, and support them as they process their sometimes volatile emotions during this process. At the end of all of this labor, some loved ones insist upon misgendering nonbinary people anyway. There is only so much that nonbinary people can control while attempting to redo gender within their relationships. This process is interactive and requires cooperation from both parties.

Even those who succeed in redoing their relationships to be more gender-affirming still encounter erasure within institutions that only acknowledge binary gender categories. I call this the "binary box dilemma" and analyze it through the framework of "symbolic annihilation"—that is, the systematic omission, trivialization, or condemnation of a group of people. Nonbinary people find themselves forcefully sorted into one of these two binary boxes in a range of institutional arenas, including the workplace and universities, the medical system, and even while pursuing services that have no reason to ask about gender, such as entertainment streaming accounts. There are very few opportunities to fight back against this institutional erasure of nonbinary gender. However, some people do try, taking on such tasks as writing to administrators and filing complaints with receptionists. Occasionally, these limited opportunities to fight back are received by well-positioned allies who recognize the validity of nonbinary people's complaints and adjust the institution's gender scheme accordingly. However, these anecdotes remain the exception that proves the rule of gender diversity's ongoing erasure at the institutional level.

I acknowledge that gender recognition is not always desired or safe for nonbinary people. I discuss this reality by highlighting how nonbinary people strategically avoid situations and places that feel unsafe. Unfortunately, as we saw, the looming threat of gender violence cannot always be so easily predicted or avoided. Malicious strangers who recognize nonbinary people for being out of place within the gender binary system often take it upon themselves to punish nonbinary people for their deviance, thereby effectively holding them accountable to the gender binary system. Therefore, while exhaustion and emotional management are salient concerns among my interviewees when it comes to identity management, physical safety remains a top concern as well.

These joint considerations of identity management, exhaustion management, and safety constitute the process that I call "managing difference" or in this case "managing gender difference." This is a temporal process that is shaped by society's lack of knowledge and understanding about one's identity, a process that is particular to those who have been rendered unintelligible in a certain place and time by others. As society becomes more familiar with gender diversity and able to recognize it for what it is, nonbinary people might not have to invest so much of their energy into managing their difference from society's dominant gender ideology. However, we are not there as a society quite yet.

This is hardly the first book to theorize identity management or even more specifically, the "coming out" process. But I believe that the case of nonbinary gender contributes something new and special to this theoretical project. This case study illuminates how difficult it is to achieve social recognition when your identity directly challenges the dominant cultural ideology and worldview. The hope for any such minority group is that the general public will become more educated about their identity over time without placing the burden on them to be the educators. But to get to that destination, allies must step up. Allies can channel our cis privilege toward educating the public, without having to fear for our physical and emotional well-being to the same degree as nonbinary people.

This is and always has been my chief motivation for writing this book—to share the explanatory burden so it becomes just a little bit lighter for nonbinary people themselves; to help spread awareness to fellow cisgender people so they will be more sensitive and receptive when someone introduces themselves along with they/them pronouns. I want people who read this book to go forth and educate other cisgender people about gender diversity. I am trying to promote and enhance what Jay Orne calls "ally consciousness."

Ally Consciousness

Certain progressive pockets within the United States have become increasingly aware and welcoming of gender diversity, but this cultural shift is still very much in progress and not sufficiently widespread to put nonbinary people's minds at ease. For this very reason, allies are incredibly important resources in this social shift. We simply do not have as much at risk when we speak up about gender diversity. We can educate other cisgender people about the fallacy of the gender binary without fearing for our own physical safety. We can field the inappropriate and triggering reactions from cisgender people when their worldview comes under fire, so they can get it out of their system and get over it. These interactions are not nearly as draining or psychologically damaging for us as they are for nonbinary people who usually perform this labor without consenting to it. The more people we educate, the easier daily life will become for nonbinary people.

A corollary can be found in literature on race, particularly on social justice activists of color who struggle with "activist burnout"[1] and "racial battle fatigue."[2] I write this in the midst of George Floyd murder protests, and white people's sudden interest and willingness to educate themselves about how to be better allies to black people. Blog articles have proliferated during this time about the fatigue, PTSD, and the emotional and explanatory burdens that people of color experience on a daily basis in this country. In response, white allies have accepted that it is our duty to engage in difficult conversations with fellow white people about the harsh realities of racism within this country. We are becoming more aware of how unfair it is to place this educational burden on Black people. It appears that the forms of labor that racial and gender minorities assume are strikingly similar. The fatigue, the propensity toward burnout, and the daily battle for recognition, all strongly parallel one another.

Several of my interviewees voice a grateful awareness of the allies who alleviate some of their "gender battle fatigue" by taking corrective or explanatory labor off their hands. Some have romantic partners who correct people during instances of misgendering. For example, Marley discussed at length how proactive their partner Krista has been in helping them secure gender recognition from others:

> I have a really hard time correcting people, especially people in positions of authority, which is kind of where my partner comes in. When she hears that she corrects them for me. I think it comes off better if someone else says you know, "Marley doesn't use female pronouns. Marley uses 'they' pronouns because they don't identify as a woman." Having someone else speak up I think legitimizes it in a way that me speaking up for myself doesn't.

Marley is gratefully aware of the power that cis allies wield in legitimizing nonbinary gender, though this power allocation is obviously problematic. And yet, it is a documented reality within many minoritized groups' fights for equal rights. For example, feminine women are perceived as more objective and persuasive when discussing the need for feminism than masculine-presenting women.[3] Similarly, men within gender studies profit off of their allegedly unbiased ability to persuade audiences that feminism is good for everyone, including men, while women who do this same work go unrecognized and undercompensated.[4] This pattern demonstrates that when people who wield social privilege and benefit from the status quo align themselves with efforts to advance social change, reluctant onlookers (who likely identify with the privileged ally in question) are more likely to listen and reconsider their investment in the status quo as well.

These allies can invest energy into educating the public without worrying about the same burnout concerns that members of the oppressed community experience. Krista, for example, has had a number of vexing conversations with her parents when Marley is not present: "Her mother asked her something along the lines of, 'So if you guys have kids does that mean that they'll have to have 'they' pronouns too?' She's like, 'No. Our kids will use whatever pronouns they want to and that has nothing to do with them. I don't understand why you make that connection.'" Krista assumes the responsibility to educate her mother behind the scenes about Marley's gender and about nonbinary gender more generally. This energy investment ultimately saves Marley the time and emotional fatigue involved in explaining why one person's gender does not determine another person's gender. Krista even assumes this explanatory labor in Marley's workplace, since Marley is unbearably uncomfortable with confrontation:

> I'm interning at a church this year, which is very fascinating. They are very good with binary trans people. But they have no idea what they're doing with me. So, I've had to explain to all of the clerical staff what "they" pronouns are

and how they work and what being nonbinary means. And actually, Krista has done a fair amount of that explaining and does a much better job of it than I do. She's a wonderful, wonderful advocate.

Marley knows that their workplace is receptive to gender diversity in theory, but they need a lot of coaching in practice. Marley successfully mustered the courage to assert themselves initially, but they are overwhelmed by the following tasks of reminding and coaching their colleagues. This is where their partner steps in and advocates on their behalf.

In addition to partners, parents of interviewees have pleasantly surprised them through their advocacy efforts. Although Kennedy felt hurt and dismissed by their mother when they first "came out" to her, their mother has since transformed into a proactive ally: "Like, she asked me a while ago 'Should I correct people? I don't know,' so I was like, 'Yeah! You should!' And she was like, 'Oh! Okay.' And now she will." Similarly, Reagan's father has been taking the initiative to adjust his language when referring to Reagan in conversations with other people:

> One time we were just walking the dogs and he—out of the blue, we weren't even talking—he was like, "So how do I introduce you to people?" And I was glad that he asked, 'cause he wouldn't know otherwise. 'Cause he loves to say "This is my daughter." He's just so, so proud to say that! And I was like, "You can just say 'This is Reagan.' You don't have to like, define the relationship, but if you want to define the relationship, you can say 'This is my child' or 'This is my kid' or..." and he's like, "Okay." And so, he's been doing a really, really, really good job and I'm really appreciative that he's trying so hard.

Reagan was deeply touched that their father was clearly investing significant thought into how to honor their gender transition. Moreover, this conversation established that their father is committed to gendering them properly in interactions with other cisgender people. To extend the battle metaphor, Reagan's father has situated himself beside his child, on the frontlines of the gender revolution. He is ready to show up and fight for his child's right to be seen.

Even some employers are developing their ally consciousness and investing labor into recognizing gender diversity in the workplace. Justice hadn't planned on disclosing their gender or pronouns at work, until their employer surprised them by signaling her ally status:

> My boss came up to me and was like, "Hey, I know you're in the queer community and I wanted to ask you, like, how to go about using 'they/them' pronouns

with Sy? What happens if I fuck up, what do I do?" And I spoke to her about it, like, "Just so you know, if you fuck up, that's okay, just be accountable. And it's okay to fuck up in the beginning." And at the same time, I was like, "Also, just so you are aware, I also would like the they/them pronoun to be used at work." And she was like, "Oh! Okay great!"

Justice's employer had already begun to rethink the relationship between sex and gender, as well as the gender system itself, in part because of her exposure to other nonbinary people. This burgeoning consciousness made it easier for Justice to "out" themselves, since it didn't require follow-up explanatory labor. In this case, the "coming out" experience for a nonbinary person was as straightforward as it is for gay or lesbian people; the disclosure was the beginning and the end of the "coming out" interaction.

Justice's encounter with their boss also highlights another main point that I desperately hope my cisgender readers will remember long after finishing this book, which is that you *do* know nonbinary (and trans) people even if you don't know that you do. It is up to you to really think about why they don't feel sufficiently safe about disclosing their gender to you. Justice's employer didn't realize that she had not one but several nonbinary employees until she started to work on herself and broadcast that she was committed to redoing gender at work.

When cisgender people are open-minded and receptive to social change, they can become powerfully efficacious allies to nonbinary people. As I said, I imagine this as a ripple-effect phenomenon, with nonbinary gender disclosure as the impactful moment that spreads outwards, causing more and more cisgender allies to rethink and redo gender themselves. Rhiannon alluded to this process when they explained that they historically assumed more explanatory labor than they wanted to in the hopes that it would save some other nonbinary person from getting misgendered in the future. And indeed, we have seen plentiful evidence of this ripple effect in action throughout the pages of this book, such as when K's father asked how they would like to be referenced after they give birth. The more people meet or learn about nonbinary people, the stronger ally consciousness will become within our society.

That being said, well-meaning allies can still unintentionally do more harm than good. It is critically important to respect people's safety considerations and not accidentally "out" them. Many interviewees within this book are "out" to friends and teachers, but not to their parents, for example. They are trusting those teachers to respect their name and pronoun specifications in class, but not in communication with their parents. There are also people who are "out" to their friends, but not in the workplace. In academic terms, outness is often "field-contingent."

So, what are allies supposed to do with this knowledge? Rhiannon was pleasantly surprised when their cisgender friends asked them this very question: "When you get misgendered in the classroom, do you want me to speak up? Or do you want me to, like, talk to the person afterwards or speak up in the moment?" Riley has also encountered this sensitivity, though mainly within their "queer bubble": "I don't correct people, but it's been a conversation I have with other queer people, where they asked me, 'To what extent would you like me to correct other people? How important is this to you, and in what spaces?' And I'm just so grateful to have such incredible friends." My readers might be frustrated to learn that there is no one answer to this question about when to linguistically acknowledge a friend's nonbinary gender and when to strategically misgender them—it varies from person to person. But in order to actually be an ally—and not just go through the motions of performative allyship—we must do our best to remember and respect the limitations of people's outness. As Morgan said, "They don't have to get it, they just have to respect me." You do not want to be the person who costs a nonbinary friend an employment opportunity or gets them kicked out of their home. Just remember that your nonbinary friend might feel weird about asking you to remember these parameters unless you directly request further directions and thus signal that you are willing to invest the labor.

Nonbinary people are by no means obligated to tell other people about their gender, especially if they feel unsafe or too emotionally brittle. However, every time they do decide to disclose their gender to cisgender people, public awareness of gender diversity increases. The amount of cisgender people who are "in the wise" grows. And as a consequence, the explanatory burden gets distributed among more people, leaving less of it for nonbinary people themselves to carry.

Social change is undoubtedly afoot. The parameters of socially permitted and recognized gender expression and identities have expanded. According to a Pew research poll in 2018,[5] seventy-five percent of Generation Z respondents have heard about people who use gender-neutral pronouns and one-third know someone who has clarified that they use a gender-neutral pronoun. Half think there should be more options on surveys than just man or woman and half say society should be more accepting of people who do not identify as a woman or a man. This growing awareness is not just limited to the youngest generation—Millennials report similar sentiments and levels of awareness. Even half of the Baby Boomers surveyed have at least heard of people using gender-neutral pronouns. These findings also indicate that people who know someone who uses a gender-neutral pronoun are more comfortable with the practice of using gender-neutral pronouns moving forward. Evidently, the microscale interactions as noted within this book are having a direct impact on public acceptance. Regressive forces can criticize and lament these social changes as much as they want, but it won't stop the ripples from spreading. Ally consciousness is expanding wider with each subsequent generation.

This seemingly microscale ripple-effect phenomenon is having an impact well beyond the interpersonal level. When people in positions of power develop ally consciousness—or more cynically, feel pressure to at least perform ally consciousness—the redoing of gender can happen at the institutional level as well. Indeed, institutions are beginning to recognize gender diversity. Even when I wrote this in 2020, toy stores such as Target, Amazon, Toys 'R' Us, and Kmart had removed gender assignments from toy categories. Brands such as Abercrombie and Fitch, H&M, John Lewis, Nununu, and Target had begun to offer gender-neutral options for clothing. Facebook enabled users to write in their gender instead of choosing pre-selected gender categories. *The Washington Post* recognized the validity of "they/them/their" as a gender-neutral singular pronoun. *The L.A. Times* recognized the gender-neutral honorific "Mx" alongside Mr., Mrs, and Ms. And *Merriam-Webster Dictionary* added Mx. as an entry. By the time this book is published, the list of examples will be exponentially longer.

Even at the most inflexible level of institutional accountability, gender had already begun to expand by 2020. Austria, Australia, Canada, Denmark, Germany, India, the Netherlands, Nepal, New Zealand, Pakistan, the Philippines, Thailand, the United Kingdom, the United States, and Uruguay had all made strides in recent years toward institutionally recognizing the existence of more than two genders. Australia, New Zealand, Pakistan, and Canada all enabled people to file for nonbinary gender markers on their passports. California, Washington, Oregon, Colorado, New York City, and New Jersey had all passed measures to allow nonbinary gender markers on birth certificates. California, Oregon, Washington D.C., New York City, Maine, Minnesota, Arkansas, Massachusetts, and Colorado also enabled people to select nonbinary gender markers on their driver's licenses and state-issued IDs. Gender-neutral single-stall bathrooms became a requirement under state law in California. 267 colleges and universities in the United States had instituted gender-inclusive on-campus housing policies that allow people to select roommates of any gender. Ten historically "all-women's" colleges extended enrollment to nonbinary students. And again—the list will be much longer by the time you read this book. These institutional shifts reflect the beginning of an irreversible societal awakening and a redoing—or expansion—of gender on a grand scale.

Of course, the three levels of accountability within the "doing gender" model can never be entirely separated from one another. When the next generation comes of age, surrounded by these gender-diverse options in their interpersonal and institutional interactions, they will contingently learn about the possibility of identifying beyond the gender binary at an earlier age. Thus, conceivably, the next generation will be able to save some of the time, energy, and emotions that the identity "flowchart" consumes. Instead of happening upon nonbinary as a default at the end of a long and isolating identity crisis, the next generation might simply always know about nonbinary as a standard gender category that is presented routinely next to "woman" and "man" on forms and surveys.

As society becomes a safer place for nonbinary people and more people "come out" as a result, we will likely see a change in the interactional processes that currently accompany the nonbinary "coming out" process. This book simply captures a moment in time at the beginning of society's acknowledgment of gender diversity. My hope is that these observations and analyses will be helpful for people who study nonbinary gender and social change more generally, but I also know that the field is rapidly expanding alongside increasing awareness of gender diversity. Ever since I began this research project in 2014, there has been a marked blossoming of research, media representation, and general knowledge about nonbinary people. Transgender Studies as a discipline has begun to encourage more research on the gender diversity within that umbrella term and the "doing gender" canon has continued to push for more of a focus on transgender and queer people. Researchers who study nonbinary gender in the future will have a wealth of studies to draw upon while formulating their theories and observations. Undoubtedly, these studies will enhance and complicate the observations made in this book, and draw upon larger data sets with more racial diversity, possibly situated in other cultural and national contexts. All of this is good. This is intellectual progress.

Just as academics have turned much more attention to nonbinary gender since 2014, so too has the mainstream media. This element of media representation is crucial because it reaches the entire general population, whether or not everyone in that population embraces social change. Regardless of people's feelings about nonbinary gender, I'd wager many more people have at least heard of it now. I earnestly hope that this book, which has centered so many nonbinary people's voices, intimate thoughts, and experiences, has helped my cisgender readers to rethink gender, reconsider their investment in the binary gender system, and join the other cisgender allies who are showing up to help our battle-beleaguered nonbinary friends. This gender revolution has not passively happened. It is an ongoing fight, that frees everyone to be and "do" their gender as authentically as possible. It's time to join ranks and march together into a boundless future.

Notes

1. Gorski (2015), Plyler (2006), Gomes (1992), Chen and Gorski (2015), and Gorski and Chen (2015).
2. Smith et al. (2007), Arnold et al. (2016), and Smith (2004).
3. Bullock and Fernald (2003).
4. See Leek (2019) for feminist resistance to "men-streaming".
5. Pew Research Poll 2018, "Gen Z Looks a Lot Like Millennials on Key Social and Political Issues." Pew Research Center. https://www.pewsocialtrends.org/2019/01/17/generation-z-looks-a-lot-like-millennials-on-key-social-and-political-issues/.

Demographics Table

#	Pseudonym	Age	Race/ ethnicity	Assigned Sex	Pronoun	Gender label	Trans
1	Addison	26	white	AFAB	ze/they	gq/ nb	Y/N
2	Alex	26	white	AMAB	they	nb/gq	Y
3	Ashton	23	white	AFAB	they	nb	Y/N
4	Avery	28	white	AMAB	he/they	gq/nb	N
5	Cameron	20	white	AMAB	they/them	nb	Y /N
6	Carson	29	white	AFAB	they	agender	Y
7	Carter	20	white	AMAB	they	nb/ gq/ agender	Y
8	Casey	27	white	AFAB	she/ hen	nb/ gq/ agender	Y/N
9	Cleopatra	23	Yemenite	AMAB	they	genderfluid/ nb/ questioning	Y
10	Corey	28	white Jewish	AFAB	they	nb	Y
11	Dakota	31	white	AMAB	they	nb/ gq	Y
12	Devin	24	Romani	intersex	they	nb	Y
13	Donna	28	white	AFAB	they	genderfluid/ no label	Y
14	Drew	23	white Jewish	AMAB	they	gender questioning	N
15	Emerson	19	white	AFAB	they/ she	nb/ genderfluid	Y/N
16	Harley	30	white	AFAB	she/ her	gq/ nb/ androgynous	N
17	Hayden	21	white	AFAB	they	genderfluid	Y/N
18	Hunter	19	mixed- black, white, NA	AFAB	his/ their	genderfluid	Y

(continued)

© The Editor(s) (if applicable) and The Author(s), under exclusive
license to Springer Nature Switzerland AG 2022
H. Darwin, *Redoing Gender*,
https://doi.org/10.1007/978-3-030-83617-7

(continued)

#	Pseudonym	Age	Race/ ethnicity	Assigned Sex	Pronoun	Gender label	Trans
19	Jack	26	white	AFAB	they	nb/ gq/ trans-masculine(ish)	Y/N
20	Jayden	23	white	AMAB	they	genderfluid	Y
21	Jaylen	25	white	AFAB	she/her	gq	Y/N
22	Jesse	26	white Jewish	AFAB	they	nb	Y
23	Jes	24	white	AFAB	hen/him/they	nb	Y/N
24	Justice	26	Native American, Latinx (Guatemalan)	AFAB	themme	two-spirited	N
25	K	30	white	AFAB	they/she	nb/gq	Y/N
26	Kai	25	white	AFAB	they	gq/nb	N
27	Kazi	20	Bengali	AFAB	they/him	gq/ nb/ androgynous	Y
28	Kennedy	21	white	AMAB	they	agender/ nb/ gq	Y/N
29	Lane	24	white	AFAB	they/he	nb	Y
30	Lisa	61	white	AMAB	she/ he	Gq	Y
31	Logan	35	white/ Scottish	AFAB	they	Nb	Y/N
32	Marley	24	white	AFAB	they	gq/ gnc	Y/N
33	Mason	28	Asian-American	AMAB	they	Gq	N
34	Morgan	22	white	AFAB	they	Nb	Y
35	Parker	29	Phillipino	AMAB	any	nb/ gq/ gnc	N
36	Peyton	29	white	AMAB	any	gq/ genderfuck/ gnc	Y
37	Phoenix	29	white	AFAB	they	nb femme, avoids labels: queer/ nb/ gq/ trans-feminine	N
38	Piper	22	Arabic	AFAB	they	nb/ gq	Y
39	Reagan	32	white	AFAB	they	nb/ gq	Y
40	Reese	21	white	AMAB	they/he	gq / masc of center/ queer man	Y/N
41	Rhiannon	24	white	AFAB	they/she	grey-gender/ nb	N
42	Riley	27	white	AMAB	they	gq/ nb/ two-spirit/ no label	N
43	River	34	white	AFAB		gq/nb	Y/N
44	Rowan	22	mixed- black and Phillipinx	AFAB	they	nb/ gq	
45	Sam	35	white	AFAB	any	nb/ gq/ two-spirit	Y/N

(continued)

(continued)

#	Pseudonym	Age	Race/ ethnicity	Assigned Sex	Pronoun	Gender label	Trans
46	Sequoia	21	Latinx/Middle-Eastern	AFAB	they/ze	genderfluid (gendero fluido), gq, nb	Y/N
47	Sydney	32	white	AFAB	they	Nb	

References

Acker, Joan. 2006. Inequality Regimes: Gender, Class, and Race in Organizations. *Gender & Society* 20 (4): 441–464.

Ahlsen, Birgitte, Hilde Bondevik, Anne Marit Mengshoel, and Kari Nyheim Solbrække. 2014. (Un)Doing Gender in a Rehabilitation Context: A Narrative Analysis of Gender and Self in Stories of Chronic Muscle Pain. *Disability and Rehabilitation* 36 (5): 359–366.

Alexander, Jonathan. 2002. Homo-Pages and Queer Sites: Studying the Construction and Representation of Queer Identities on the World Wide Web. *International Journal of Sexuality and Gender Studies* 7 (2–3): 85–106.

Anderson, Eric. 2010. *Inclusive Masculinity: The Changing Nature of Masculinities*. New York: Routledge.

Arnold, Noelle Witherspoon, Emily R. Crawford, and Muhammad Khalifa. 2016. Psychological Heuristics and Faculty of Color: Racial Battle Fatigue and Tenure/Promotion. *The Journal of Higher Education* 87 (6): 890–919.

Ashford, Chris. 2009. Queer Theory, Cyber-Ethnographies and Researching Online Sex Environments. *Information and Communications Technology Law* 18 (3): 297–314.

Avishai, Orit. 2008. "Doing Religion" in a Secular World: Women in Conservative Religions and the Question of Agency. *Gender & Society* 22 (4): 409–433.

Barbee, Harry, and Douglas Schrock. 2019. Un/Gendering Social Selves: How Nonbinary People Navigate and Experience a Binarily Gendered World. *Sociological Forum* 34 (3): 572–593.

Basow, Susan A. 1991. Women and their Body Hair. *Psychology of Women Quarterly* 15 (1): 83–96.

Bianchi, Suzanne M., Melissa A. Milkie, Liana C. Sayer, and John P. Robinson. 2000. Is Anyone Doing the Housework? Trends in the Gender Division of Household Labor. *Social Forces* 79 (1): 191–228.

Bird, Sharon R. 1996. Welcome to the Men's Club: Homosociality and the Maintenance of Hegemonic Masculinity. *Gender & Society* 10 (2): 120–132.

Bittman, Michael, Paula England, Liana Sayer, Nancy Folbre, and George Matheson. 2003. When Does Gender Trump Money? Bargaining and Time in Household Work. *American Journal of Sociology* 109 (1): 186–214.

Blair, Karen L., and Rhea Ashley Hoskin. 2015. Experiences of Femme Identity: Coming Out, Invisibility and Femmephobia. *Psychology & Sexuality* 6 (3): 229–244.

Bolton, Sharon. 2004. Conceptual Confusions: Emotion Work as Skilled Work. *The Skills That Matter* 19: 37.

Bradley, Evan D., Julia Salkind, Ally Moore, and Sofi Teitsort. 2019. Singular 'They' and Novel Pronouns: Gender-Neutral, Nonbinary, or Both? *Proceedings of the Linguistic Society of America* 4 (1): 36–41.

Brines, Julie. 1994. Economic Dependency, Gender, and the Division of Labor at Home. *American Journal of Sociology* 100 (3): 652–688.

Browne, Kath. 2004. Genderism and the Bathroom Problem: (Re)Materialising Sexed Sites Recreating Sexed Bodies. *Gender, Place & Culture* 11 (3): 331–346.

Brumbaugh-Johnson, Stacey M., and Kathleen E. Hull. 2019. Coming Out as Transgender: Navigating the Social Implications of a Transgender Identity. *Journal of Homosexuality* 66 (8): 1148–1177.

Bruni, Attila, Silvia Gherardi, and Barbara Poggio. 2004. Entrepreneur-Mentality, Gender and the Study of Women Entrepreneurs. *Journal of Organizational Change Management* 17 (3): 256–268.

Bucholtz, Mary, and Kira Hall. 2005. Identity and Interaction: A Sociocultural Linguistic Approach. *Discourse Studies* 7 (4–5): 585–614.

Budgeon, Shelley. 2014. The Dynamics of Gender Hegemony: Femininities Masculinities and Social Change. *Sociology* 48 (2): 317–334.

Bullock, Heather E., and Julian L. Fernald. 2003. "Feminism Lite?" Feminist Identification, Speaker Appearance, and Perceptions of Feminist and Antifeminist Messengers. *Psychology of Women Quarterly* 27 (4): 291–299.

Butler, Judith. 2004. *Undoing Gender*. Hove: Psychology Press.

Caldwell, Kia Lilly. 2003. "Look at Her Hair": The Body Politics of Black Womanhood in Brazil. *Transforming Anthropology* 11: 2.

Callis, April Scarlette. 2014. Bisexual, Pansexual, Queer: Non-Binary Identities and the Sexual Borderlands. *Sexualities* 17 (1–2): 63–80.

Campbell, John E. 2004. *Getting It on Online: Cyberspace, Gay Male Sexuality, and Embodied Identity*. Binghamton, NY: Harrington Park Press.

Cass, Vivienne C. 1979. Homosexuality Identity Formation: A Theoretical Model. *Journal of Homosexuality* 4 (3): 219–235.

Cass, Vivienne C. 1984. Homosexual Identity Formation: Testing a Theoretical Model. *Journal of Sex Research* 20 (2): 143–167.

Catalano, D. Chase J. 2015. "Trans Enough?" The Pressures Trans Men Negotiate in Higher Education. *Transgender Studies Quarterly* 2 (3): 411–430.

Cavanagh, Sheila L. 2011. You are Where You Urinate. *The Gay & Lesbian Review* 18 (4): 18–20

Charmaz, Kathy. 2006. The Power of Names. *Journal of Contemporary Ethnography* 35 (4): 396–399.

Chen, Cher Weixia, and Paul C. Gorski. 2015. Burnout in Social Justice and Human Rights Activists: Symptoms, Causes and Implications. *Journal of Human Rights Practice* 7 (3): 366–390.

Clements, Angela. 2009. Sexual Orientation, Gender Nonconformity, and Trait-Based Discrimination: Cautionary Tales from Title VII & (and) an Argument for Inclusion. *Berkeley Journal of Gender, Law & Justice* 24: 166.

Coates, Jennifer. 1986. *Women, Men and Language: A Sociolinguistic Account of Gender Differences in Language*. London: Longman.

Coleman, Eli. 1982. Developmental Stages of the Coming Out Process. *Journal of Homosexuality* 7 (2–3): 31–43.

Connell, Raewyn W. 1987. *Gender and Power*. Cambridge, UK: Cambridge University Press.

Connell, Robert William. 1992. A Very Straight Gay: Masculinity, Homosexual Experience, and the Dynamics of Gender. *American Sociological Review*: 735–751.

Connell, Robert W. 1995. *Masculinities: Knowledge, Power and Social Change*. Berkeley and Los Angeles: University of California Press.

Connell, Raewyn. 2009. Accountable Conduct: "Doing Gender" in Transsexual and Political Retrospect. *Gender & Society* 23 (1): 104–111.

Correll, Shelley J. 2001. Gender and the Career Choice Process: The Role of Biased Self-Assessments. *American Journal of Sociology* 106 (6): 1691–1730.

Craig, Maxine Leeds. 2002. *Ain't I a Beauty Queen?: Black Women, Beauty, and the Politics of Race*. New York: Oxford University Press.

De Beauvoir, Simone. 1973. *The Second Sex*. New York: Vintage Books.

Darwin, Helana. 2017a. Doing Gender Beyond the Binary: A Virtual Ethnography. *Symbolic Interaction* 40 (3): 317–334.

Darwin, H. 2017b. The Pariah Femininity Hierarchy: Comparing White Women's Body Hair and Fat Stigmas in the United States. *Gender, Place & Culture* 24 (1): 135–146.

Darwin, Helana. 2018. Redoing Gender, Redoing Religion. *Gender & Society* 32 (3): 348–370.

Darwin, H. 2020. Navigating the Religious Gender Binary. *Sociology of Religion* 81 (2): 185–205.

Davidson, M. 2007. Seeking Refuge Under the Umbrella: Inclusion, Exclusion, and Organizing Within the Category Transgender. *Sexuality Research & Social Policy: A Journal of the NSRC* 4 (4): 60–80.

Davis, Georgiann. 2015. *Contesting Intersex: The Dubious Diagnosis*, vol. 10. New York: New York University Press.

Deutsch, Francine M. 2007. Undoing Gender. *Gender & Society* 21 (1): 106–127.

Devor, Holly. 1989. *Gender Blending: Confronting the Limits of Duality*, vol. 533. Bloomington: Indiana University Press.

Doan, Petra L. 2010. The Tyranny of Gendered Spaces–Reflections from Beyond the Gender Dichotomy. *Gender, Place & Culture* 17 (5): 635–654.

Dubin, Samuel, Sari Reisner, Eric W. Schrimshaw, Asa Radix, Aisha Khan, Salem Harry-Hernandez, Sophia A. Zweig, Liadh Timmins, and Dustin T. Duncan. 2021. Public Restrooms in Neighborhoods and Public Spaces: A Qualitative Study of Transgender and Nonbinary Adults in New York City. *Sexuality Research and Social Policy*: 1–11.

Duesterhaus, Megan, Liz Grauerholz, Rebecca Weichsel, and Nicholas A. Guittar. 2011. The Cost of Doing Femininity: Gendered Disparities in Pricing of Personal Care Products and Services. *Gender Issues* 28 (4): 175–191.

Eisner, Shiri. 2013. *Bi: Notes for a Bisexual Revolution*. Berkeley, CA: Seal Press.

Ellis, Havelock. 1911. *Studies in the Psychology of Sex*, vol. 6. Philadelphia: FA Davis.

Factor, Rhonda, and Esther Rothblum. 2008. Exploring Gender Identity and Community Among Three Groups of Transgender Individuals in the United States: MTFs, FTMs, and Genderqueers. *Health Sociology Review* 17 (3): 235–253.

Fahs, Breanne. 2011. Dreaded "Otherness" Heteronormative Patrolling in Women's Body Hair Rebellions. *Gender & Society* 25 (4): 451–472.

Faugier, Jean, and Mary Sargeant. 1997. Sampling Hard to Reach Populations. *Journal of Advanced Nursing* 26 (4): 790–797.

Feinberg, Leslie. 1996. *Transgender Warriors: Making History from Joan of Arc to Dennis Rodman*. Boston: Beacon Press.

Fenstermaker, Sarah, and Candace West. 2013. *Doing Gender, Doing Difference: Inequality, Power, and Institutional Change*. New York: Routledge.

Friedman, Asia. 2013. *Blind to Sameness: Sexpectations and the Social Construction of Male and Female Bodies*. Chicago: University of Chicago Press.

Garfinkel, Harold. 1967. *Studies in Ethnomethodology*. Englewood Cliffs, NJ: Prentice- Hall.

Garrison, Spencer. 2018. On the Limits of "Trans Enough": Authenticating Trans Identity Narratives. *Gender & Society* 32 (5): 613–637.

Gerbner, George. 1972. Violence in Television Drama: Trends and Symbolic Functions. *Television and Social Behavior* 1: 28–187.

Gimlin, Debra. 2002. *Body Work: Beauty and Self-Image in American Culture*. Berkeley: University of California Press.

Glover, Jenna A., Renee V. Galliher, and Trenton G. Lamere. 2009. Identity Development and Exploration Among Sexual Minority Adolescents: Examination of a Multidimensional Model. *Journal of Homosexuality* 56 (1): 77–101.

Goffman, Erving. 1978. *The Presentation of Self in Everyday Life*. London: Harmondsworth.

Gomes, Mary E. 1992. The Rewards and Stresses of Social Change: A Qualitative Study of Peace Activists. *Journal of Humanistic Psychology* 32 (4): 138–146.

Gorski, Paul C. 2015. Relieving Burnout and the "Martyr Syndrome" Among Social Justice Education Activists: The Implications and Effects of Mindfulness. *The Urban Review* 47 (4): 696–716.

Gorski, Paul C., and Cher Chen. 2015. "Frayed all Over:" The Causes and Consequences of Activist Burnout Among Social Justice Education Activists. *Educational Studies* 51 (5): 385–405.

Guittar, Nicholas A., and Rachel L. Rayburn. 2016. Coming Out: The Career Management of One's Sexuality. *Sexuality & Culture* 20 (2): 336–357.

Halberstam, Judith. 1998. Transgender Butch: Butch/FTM Border Wars and the Masculine Continuum. *GLQ: A Journal of Lesbian and Gay Studies* 4 (2): 287–310.

Harrison, J., J. Grant, and J.L. Herman. 2012. *A Gender Not Listed Here: Genderqueers, Gender Rebels, and Otherwise in the National Transgender Discrimination Survey*. Los Angeles, CA: eScholarship, University of California.

Harrison-Quintana, Jack, Jaime M. Grant, and Ignacio G. Rivera. 2015. Boxes of Our Own Creation a Trans Data Collection Wo/Manifesto. *TSQ: Transgender Studies Quarterly* 2 (1): 166–174.

Heimer, Karen, and Stacy De Coster. 1999. The Gendering of Violent Delinquency. *Criminology* 37 (2): 277–318.

Herzig, Rebecca M. 2015. *Plucked: A History of Hair Removal*, vol. 8. New York: New York University Press.

Hillier, Lynne, and Lyn Harrison. 2007. Building Realities Less Limited Than Their Own: Young People Practising Same-Sex Attraction on the Internet. *Sexualities* 10 (1): 82–100.

Hill, Shirley A. 2002. Teaching and Doing Gender in African American Families. *Sex Roles* 47 (11–12): 493–506.

Horowitz, Janna L., and Michael D. Newcomb. 2002. A Multidimensional Approach to Homosexual Identity. *Journal of Homosexuality* 42 (2): 1–19.

Hoskin, Rhea Ashley. 2019. Femmephobia: The Role of Anti-Femininity and Gender Policing in LGBTQ+ People's Experiences of Discrimination. *Sex Roles* 81 (11): 686–703.

Irby, Courtney Ann. 2014. Dating in Light of Christ: Young Evangelicals Negotiating Gender in the Context of Religious and Secular American Culture. *Sociology of Religion* 75 (2): 260–283.

Johnson, Austin H. 2015. Normative Accountability: How the Medical Model Influences Transgender Identities and Experiences. *Sociology Compass* 9 (9): 803–813.

Johnson, Austin H. 2016. Transnormativity: A New Concept and Its Validation through Documentary Film About Transgender Men. *Sociological Inquiry* 86 (4): 465–491.

Johnston, Josée, and Shyon Baumann. 2014. *Foodies: Democracy and Distinction in the Gourmet Foodscape*. New York: Routledge.

Kaufman, Joanne M., and Cathryn Johnson. 2004. Stigmatized Individuals and the Process of Identity. *The Sociological Quarterly* 45 (4): 807–833.

Kessler, Suzanne J., and Wendy McKenna. 1985. *Gender: An Ethnomethodological Approach*. Chicago: University of Chicago Press.

Krafft-Ebing, Richard. 1901. *Psychopathia Sexualis: With Especial Reference to Antipathic Sexual Instinct*. Keener.

Kuper, L.E., R. Nussbaum, and B. Mustanski. 2012. Exploring the Diversity of Gender and Sexual Orientation Identities in an Online Sample of Transgender Individuals. *Journal of Sex Research* 49 (2–3): 244–254.

Leek, Cliff. 2019. Understanding Feminist Resistance to "Men-Streaming." *Global Social Welfare* 6 (4): 219–229.

Leidner, Robin. 1991. Serving Hamburgers and Selling Insurance: Gender, Work, and Identity in Interactive Service Jobs. *Gender & Society* 5 (2): 154–177.

Lu, Alexander, and Y. Joel Wong. 2013. Stressful Experiences of Masculinity Among US-Born and Immigrant Asian American Men. *Gender & Society* 27 (3): 345–371.

Martin, Patricia Yancey. 2003. "Said and Done" Versus "Saying and Doing" Gendering Practices, Practicing Gender at Work. *Gender & Society* 17 (3): 342–366.

Maslach, Christina, and Susan E. Jackson. 1981. The Measurement of Experienced Burnout. *Journal of Organizational Behavior* 2 (2): 99–113.

McDowell, Linda. 2011. *Capital Culture: Gender at Work in the City*. Hoboken: Wiley.

Messerschmidt, James W. 2007. Masculinities, Crime and. *The Blackwell Encyclopedia of Sociology*.

Messerschmidt, James W. 2019. The Salience of "Hegemonic Masculinity." *Men and Masculinities* 22 (1): 85–91.

Namaste, V.K. 2000. *Invisible Lives: The Erasure of Transsexual and Transgendered People*. Chicago: University of Chicago Press.

Ndichu, Edna G., and Shikha Upadhyaya. 2019. "Going Natural": Black Women's Identity Project Shifts in Hair Care Practices. *Consumption Markets & Culture* 22 (1): 44–67.

O'brien, Rosaleen, Kate Hunt, and Graham Hart. 2005. 'It's Caveman Stuff, but That Is to a Certain Extent How Guys Still Operate': Men's Accounts of Masculinity and Help Seeking. *Social Science & Medicine* 61 (3): 503–516.

Orne, Jason. 2013. Queers in the Line of Fire: Goffman's Stigma Revisited. *The Sociological Quarterly* 54 (2): 229–253.

Oswald, Ramona Faith. 1999. Family and Friendship Relationships After Young Women Come Out as Bisexual or Lesbian. *Journal of Homosexuality* 38 (3): 65–83.

Overall, Christine. 2007. Public Toilets: Sex Segregation Revisited. *Ethics & the Environment* 12 (2): 71–91.

Pascoe, C.J. 2005. "Dude, You're a Fag": Adolescent Masculinity and the Fag Discourse. *Sexualities* 8: 329–346.

Pfeffer, Carla A. 2014. "I Don't Like Passing as a Straight Woman": Queer Negotiations of Identity and Social Group Membership. *American Journal of Sociology* 120 (1): 1–44.

Plyler, Jen. 2006. How to Keep on Keeping On: Sustaining Ourselves in Community Organizing and Social Justice Struggles. *Upping the Anti* 3: 123–134.

Pyke, Karen D., and Denise L. Johnson. 2003. Asian American Women and Racialized Femininities: "Doing" Gender Across Cultural Worlds. *Gender & Society* 17 (1): 33–53.

Rao, Aliya Hamid. 2015. Gender and Cultivating the Moral Self in Islam: Muslim Converts in an American Mosque. *Sociology of Religion* 76 (4): 413–435.

Richie, Beth. 2018. *Compelled to Crime: The Gender Entrapment of Battered, Black Women.* New York: Routledge.

Ridgeway, Cecilia L. 1997. Interaction and the Conservation of Gender Inequality: Considering Employment. *American Sociological Review*: 218–235.

Ridgeway, Cecilia L. 2009. Framed Before We Know It: How Gender Shapes Social Relations. *Gender & Society* 23 (2): 145–160.

Risman, Barbara J. 2009. From Doing to Undoing: Gender as We Know It. *Gender & Society* 23 (1): 81–84.

Risman, Barbara J. 2018. *Where the Millennials Will Take Us: A New Generation Wrestles with the Gender Structure.* New York: Oxford University Press.

Roen, Katrina. 2002. 'Either/Or' and 'Both/Neither': Discursive Tensions in Transgender Politics. *Signs* 27 (2): 501–522.

Rogers, Baker A. 2018. Drag as a Resource: Trans* and Nonbinary Individuals in the Southeastern United States. *Gender & Society* 32 (6): 889–910.

Rust, Paula C. 1993. "Coming Out" in the Age of Social Constructionism: Sexual Identity Formation Among Lesbian and Bisexual Women. *Gender & Society* 7 (1): 50–77.

Saltzburg, Susan. 2004. Learning that an Adolescent Child Is Gay or Lesbian: The Parent Experience. *Social Work* 49 (1): 109–118.

Schilt, Kristen, and Danya Lagos. 2017. The Development of Transgender Studies in Sociology. *Annual Review of Sociology* 43: 425–443.

Schilt, Kristen, and Laurel Westbrook. 2009. Doing Gender, Doing Heteronormativity: 'Gender Normals', Transgender People, and the Social Maintenance of Heterosexuality. *Gender & Society* 23 (4): 440–464.

Schippers, Mimi. 2007. Recovering the Feminine Other: Masculinity, Femininity, and Gender Hegemony. *Theory and Society* 36 (1): 85–102.

Shelton, Beth Anne, and Daphne John. 1996. The Division of Household Labor. *Annual Review of Sociology* 22 (1): 299–322.

Shuster, stef M. 2017. Punctuating Accountability: How Discursive Aggression Regulates Transgender People. *Gender & Society* 31 (4): 481–502.

Shuster, Stef M. 2019. 23. Generational Gaps or Othering the Other?

Simon, William, and John H. Gagnon. 1986. Sexual Scripts: Permanence and Change. *Archives of Sexual Behavior* 15 (2): 97–120.

Simon, William, and John H. Gagnon. 2003. Sexual Scripts: Origins, Influences and Changes. *Qualitative Sociology* 26 (4): 491–497.

Smith, William A. 2004. Black Faculty Coping with Racial Battle Fatigue: The Campus Racial Climate in a Post-Civil Rights Era. *A Long Way to Go: Conversations About Race by African American Faculty and Graduate Students* 14: 171–190.

Smith, William A., Walter R. Allen, and Lynette L. Danley. 2007. "Assume the Position... You Fit the Description" Psychosocial Experiences and Racial Battle Fatigue Among African American Male College Students. *American Behavioral Scientist* 51 (4): 551–578.

Smith, Naomi, Rebecca Wickes, and Mair Underwood. 2015. Managing a Marginalised Identity in Pro-Anorexia and Fat Acceptance Cybercommunities. *Journal of Sociology* 51 (4): 950–967.

Snow, David A., and Leon Anderson. 1987. Identity Work Among the Homeless: The Verbal Construction and Avowal of Personal Identities. *American Journal of Sociology* 92 (6): 1336–1371.

Stryker, Susan. 1998. The Transgender Issue: An Introduction. *GLQ: A Journal of Lesbian and Gay Studies* 4 (2): 145–158.

Stryker, Susan, and Paisley Currah. 2014. *General Editors' Introduction*: 303–307.

Sumerau, J. E., and Lain A.B. Mathers. 2019. *America Through Transgender Eyes.* Lanham: Rowman & Littlefield.

Sumerau, J. Edward, Ryan T. Cragun, and Lain A.B. Mathers. 2016. Contemporary Religion and the Cisgendering of Reality. *Social Currents* 3 (3): 293–311.

Sumerau, J.E., Lain A.B. Mathers, Alexandra C.H. Nowakowski, and Ryan T. Cragun. 2017. Helping Quantitative Sociology Come Out of the Closet. *Sexualities* 20 (5–6): 644–656.

Sumerau, J. E., Lain A.B. Mathers, and Dawne Moon. 2019. Foreclosing Fluidity at the Intersection of Gender and Sexual Normativities. *Symbolic Interaction.*

Synnott, Anthony. 1987. Shame and Glory: A Sociology of Hair. *The British Journal of Sociology* 38 (3): 381–413.

Tate, Shirley. 2007. Black Beauty: Shade, Hair and Anti-Racist Aesthetics. *Ethnic and Racial Studies* 30 (2): 300–319.

Testoni, Ines, and Manuela Anna Pinducciu. 2019. Grieving Those Who Still Live: Loss Experienced by Parents of Transgender Children. *Gender Studies* 18 (1): 142–162.

Thompson, Cheryl. 2009. Black Women, Beauty, and Hair as a Matter of Being. *Women's Studies* 38 (8): 831–856.

Tiggemann, Marika, and Suzanna Hodgson. 2008. The Hairlessness Norm Extended: Reasons for and Predictors of Women's Body Hair Removal at Different Body Sites. *Sex Roles* 59 (11–12): 889–897.

Toerien, Merran, Sue Wilkinson, and Precilla Y.L. Choi. 2005. Body Hair Removal: The 'Mundane' Production of Normative Femininity. *Sex Roles* 52 (5–6): 399–406.

Trautner, Mary Nell. 2005. Doing Gender, Doing Class: The Performance of Sexuality in Exotic Dance Clubs. *Gender & Society* 19 (6): 771–788.

Troiden, Dr Richard R. 1989. The Formation of Homosexual Identities. *Journal of Homosexuality* 17 (1–2): 43–74.

Tuchman, Gaye. 1979. Women's Depiction by the Mass Media. *Signs: Journal of Women in Culture and Society* 4 (3): 528–542.

Valentine, David. 2007. *Imagining Transgender: An Ethnography of a Category*. Durham, NC: Duke University Press.

Vidal-Ortiz, Salvador. 2002. Queering Sexuality and Doing Gender: Transgender Men's Identification with Gender and Sexuality. *Gender Sexualities* 6: 181–233.

Vidal-Ortiz, Salvador. 2005. Queering Sexuality and Doing Gender: Transgender Men's Identification with Gender and Sexuality. In *Gendered Sexualities*, 181–233. Bingley: Emerald Group Publishing Limited.

Vidal-Ortiz, Salvador. 2009. The Figure of the Transwoman of Color Through the Lens of "Doing Gender". *Gender & Society* 23 (1): 99–103.

Watters, John K., and Patrick Biernacki. 1989. Targeted Sampling: Options for the Study of Hidden Populations. *Social Problems* 36 (4): 416–430.

Weitz, Rose. 2011. Gender and Degendering in Autobiographical Narratives of Physical Scars. *Gender Issues* 28 (4): 192–208.

West, Candace, and Don H. Zimmerman. 1987. Doing Gender. *Gender & Society* 1 (2): 125–151.

Westbrook, Laurel. 2016. Transforming the Sex/Gender/Sexuality System. *Introducing the New Sexuality Studies*: 33–42.

Westbrook, Laurel, and Kristen Schilt. 2014. Doing Gender, Determining Gender: Transgender People, Gender Panics, and the Maintenance of the Sex/Gender/Sexuality System. *Gender & Society* 28 (1): 32–57.

Westbrook, Laurel, and Aliya Saperstein. 2015. New Categories Are Not Enough: Rethinking the Measurement of Sex and Gender in Social Surveys. *Gender & Society* 29 (4): 534–560.

Williams, Christine L. 1995. *Still a Man's World: Men who do "Women's Work."* Berkeley: University of California Press.

Wolkomir, Michelle. 2009. Making Heteronormative Reconciliations: The Story of Romantic Love, Sexuality, and Gender in Mixed-Orientation Marriages. *Gender & Society* 23 (4): 494–519.

Index